Garden Pools

Fountains & Watercourses

GARDEN POOLS FOUNTAINS & WATERCOURSES

Series Concept: Robert J. Dolezal
Encyclopedia Concept: Barbara K. Dolezal
Managing Editor: Jill Fox
Encyclopedia Writer: Kristi Hein
Water Gardening Consultant: Cash French
Photography Editor: John M. Rickard
Designer: Jerry Simon
Layout: Rik Boyd
Photoshop Artist: Gerald A. Bates
Horticulturist: Peggy Henry
Photo Stylist: Peggy Henry
Copy Editor: Barbara Coster
Proofreaders: Jane Merryman, Ken DellaPenta
Index: Aubrey McClellan, ALTA Indexing Service

President/CEO: Michael Eleftheriou
Vice President/Publisher: Linda Ball
Vice President/Retail Sales & Marketing: Kevin Haas

Home Improvement/*Gardening*
Executive Editor: Bryan Trandem
Editorial Director: Jerri Farris
Creative Director: Tim Himsel
Managing Editor: Michelle Skudlarek

Created by: Dolezal & Associates,
in partnership with Creative Publishing international, Inc.,
in cooperation with Black & Decker.
BLACK&DECKER. is a trademark of the Black & Decker
Corporation and is used under license.

Library of Congress Cataloging-in-Publication Data

Binsacca, Rich.
  Garden pools, fountains & watercourses : exciting new ideas for home
water gardens / author, Rich Binsacca ; photographer, John Rickard.
    p. cm. -- (Black & Decker outdoor home)
  ISBN 0-86573-465-8 (hardcover) -- ISBN 0-86573-466-6 (soft cover)
  1. Water gardens. 2. Water in landscape architecture. I. Title. II.
Series.
  SB423 .B58 2000
  635.9'674--dc21
                                                    00-048505

ISBN 0-86573-465-8 (hardcover)
ISBN 0-86573-466-6 (softcover)

PHOTOGRAPHY & ILLUSTRATION

PRINCIPAL PHOTOGRAPHY

JOHN M. RICKARD: Cover photograph and pgs. *iv*, *v* (upper mid L, lower mid L, & bot L), *vi*, *viii*, 2 (bot L), 3 (top R), 4, 5, 6 (mid), 8, 9, 10, 12, 13, 14, 15, 16, 17, 18, 19, 20, 21, 22, 23, 25 (step 5), 26, 27 (steps 1–3), 28, 29 (steps 1–3 & 5), 30 (top L, upper mid L, lower mid L, bot L, top R, upper mid R, & lower mid R), 31, 32 (steps 2 & 4), 33, 34, 36, 37, 38, 39, 40, 42 (inset, step 1), 43 (steps 1–2), 44, 48, 51 (steps 4–6), 52 (mid), 53, 54, 55, 56, 58, 59, 60, 61, 62, 63, 64 (steps 1–2), 65, 66, 68, 69, 70, 71, 72 (top), 75 (bot R), 76, 77, 78, 80 (bot), 81 (top & mid), 84 (top), 85 (mid & bot), 86 (mid & bot), 87 (top), 88 (mid), 89 (mid & bot), 91 (top & mid), 92, 95 (top), 97 (top & bot), 98 (mid & bot), 99 (top), 100 (top), 101 (bot), 104 (mid), 106 (top), 107 (mid), 108 (bot) 109 (top & bot), 110 (top), 111, 112 (mid), 114

OTHER PHOTOGRAPHY AND ILLUSTRATION

AQUASCAPE DESIGNS, INC.: pg. 75 (steps 1–4)

TIM BUTLER: pg. 82 (mid), 91 (bot), 113 (mid & bot)

DOUG DEALEY: pg. 3 (mid L)

ROBERT J. DOLEZAL: pgs. *v* (top L), 41, 42 (steps 2–5), 43 (steps 3-5), 45, 47, 49, 51 (steps 1–3), 108 (top)

REED ESTABROOK: pgs. 64 (steps 3–4), 73, 74

IMAGE POINT: pg. 93 (mid)

DONNA KRISCHAN: pgs. 72 (mid & bot), 81 (bot), 82 (top & bot), 87 (mid & bot), 88 (bot), 89 (top), 93 (bot), 98 (top), 101 (mid), 102 (mid), 103 (bot), 106 (mid), 112 (top & bot)

CHARLES NUCCI: pg. 85 (top)

JERRY PAVIA: pgs. 6 (bot L), 52 (bot R), 80 (mid), 83 (mid & bot), 84 (mid & bot), 88 (top), 93 (top), 94, 95 (mid & bot), 96 (mid & bot), 97 (mid), 99 (mid & bot), 100 (bot), 101 (top), 103 (top & mid), 104 (top & bot), 105, 106 (bot), 107 (top & bot), 109 (mid), 110 (mid & bot), 113 (top)

JACQUELINE RAMSEYER: pgs. 2 (top R), 3 (bot)

CHARLES SLAY: pgs. 46, 80 (top), 83 (top), 86 (top), 90, 96 (top), 100 (mid), 102 (top & bot)

YVONNE WILLIAMS: pg. 7

ILLUSTRATIONS: HILDEBRAND DESIGN

SPECIAL THANKS AND APPRECIATION IS EXPRESSED TO GREG WITTSTOCK AND AQUASCAPES DESIGNS, INC., BATAVIA, ILLINOIS FOR THEIR CONTRIBUTION TO THIS BOOK

ACKNOWLEDGEMENTS

The editors acknowledge with grateful appreciation the contribution to this book of Alden Lane Nursery, Livermore, California; Luther Burbank Home and Gardens, Santa Rosa, California; McAllister Water Gardens, Yountville, California; Wedekinds Garden Center, Sonoma, California; and Windy Oaks Aquatics, Eagle, Wisconsin; and to the following individuals: John and Karen Delaney, Norman Nather, Betsy Niles, and Rick Osborne.

Garden Pools Fountains & Watercourses

Author
Rich Binsacca

Photographer
John M. Rickard

Series Concept
Robert J. Dolezal

CREATIVE
PUBLISHING
international

Minnetonka, Minnesota

CONTENTS

INSTALLATION AND CONSTRUCTION

Page 35

PLANTING AQUATIC ENVIRONMENTS

Page 57

WATER GARDEN CARE

Page 67

ENCYCLOPEDIA OF AQUATIC PLANTS

Page 79

An outstanding selection of 93 popular and widely available aquatic and shoreline plants pictured in full-color photographs. Plants for all climate conditions and plant hardiness zones, from tender tropicals to hardy perennials. Useful information in six categories guide choice, planting, and care.

RESOURCES AND INDEX

Page 115

INTRODUCTION

My first experience with a garden pool was when I fell into one at my hometown nursery. I was about nine, I guess, all curious and awkward, exploring anything I could hoist myself onto, over, or through. The wide, flat paving stones encircling the enticing, raised pool proved a challenge for such an adventurous spirit; I suddenly found myself waist-deep with the lily pads and koi, and I went home in soggy shoes.

I've always been attracted to water, particularly the sound of it. I can listen for hours to the pounding of the ocean or a waterfall. Most of the photographs I've taken of nature include water—a raging river, a quiet lake at dawn, a mountain stream, even a trickle of runoff down the street where I grew up, or of my son splashing the water of my aunt's birdbath. I'm sure it was an unconscious effort. The water itself compelled me.

*Everybody needs
beauty as well as bread,
places to play in
and pray in, where
Nature may heal and cheer
and give strength
to body and soul alike.*

JOHN MUIR

Because water is essential for life, it evokes instinctual emotions when we are in its presence. Both children and adults will reach out to touch a ribbon-like waterfall or a bubbling fountain and pause to reflect in a peaceful garden pond. Wildlife, given the right circumstances, will make it a home.

The most enjoyable aspect of writing this book was exploring all of the things that can be done with water to elicit and achieve those experiences. Adding the sights, sounds, and feel of water in a garden is a creative endeavor that brings great rewards.

There are so many options, ranging from assembling the most basic kits to building complex projects, from simple garden pools to lush dramatic features. For me, the sight of a container brimming with water and aquatic plants just outside my front door refreshes my spirit, and the stream I'm now planning for my backyard soon will be a world of discovery and wonder for my two young boys and their friends—and for me.

With this book, I hope you'll find the water garden that brings you similar joy and personal satisfaction.

T

he presence of water is essential to any human community. People always made their homes near sources of water, in order to survive. Villages grew around streams, and communities prospered around the town well. For centuries, in homes large and small, the fountain or well was the center of outdoor activity. Outdoor water's importance was reduced after indoor plumbing was introduced, yet it remained a fundamental feature in gardens throughout the world, regardless of culture or climate.

> **People are drawn by instinct to the sight and sound of water in the garden**

More than any other garden element, water stimulates the senses of sight, sound, smell, and touch. It provides movement in the garden, as with a stream, canal, or the rippling reflection of a still pool. It offers an oasis and a shelter, cooling the body with a simple touch of mist from a fountain while protecting and nurturing a vast ecosystem of plants and wildlife.

Minimal modern pools, architectural watercourses, and fountains, as well as traditional ponds, streams, and waterfalls, comprise water features. Some features lend themselves to the symmetry of a formal garden, others are casual and mimic nature in their spontaneity. Your choice of a water feature should match your personal style, comfort level, and location. Add aquatic plants to these features and you create a water garden.

Beautiful Water Gardens

Many water features also support fish. All the design and building techniques described here are useful for establishing a suitable environment for freshwater fish. Expertise concerning the specifics of water quality, aquatic plants for a fish pond, and fish care, however, should be sought elsewhere.

Throughout this book you'll find many possibilities for creating a water feature and garden. This chapter describes the various categories of water gardens and provides examples of options within each of those general types. From simple to complex, natural to urbane, you can create a water garden that suits your personality, your home, and your purpose.

A landscape with a water feature brings new, exciting elements to your garden. Besides the ever-moving patterns found in their ripples and reflections, water gardens include a host of aquatic plants, fish, and other water creatures.

SELF-CONTAINED WATER GARDENS

A self-contained water garden is much like a flowering plant in a planter or other large container: it's a microcosm of a larger garden. Self-contained water gardens offer you several benefits over more open environments. First, they bring a structural feature, aquatic plants, and even wildlife into the smallest garden setting, such as a balcony or a small section of patio. Second, they make those elements more approachable and provide closer views, especially when the feature is located near the home or outdoor entertainment area. Imagine the impact of even the simplest self-contained water feature —a clay dish filled with rainwater—serving as a neighborhood birdbath in a spot just outside your kitchen window.

In an open setting, a self-contained water garden can be a signature element at the end of a shaded or meandering path, or it can provide a unifying point between two more formal garden areas. Because most container water features are mobile, they can be shifted in and out of the hot sun, or removed from unseasonably cold conditions, which can affect both the quality of the water and the health of the plants.

(Top) A self-contained water garden may adopt an Asian theme, as with the creative use of bamboo and textures to evoke strong linear movement in contrast to the graceful texture and restful color of spurge.

(Bottom) Water gardens are a good choice for indoor placement in sunny window locations with indirect sunlight. Supplement with artificial plant lights in locations with less than five hours per day of strong sunlight.

Self-contained water features take many forms. A formal garden may call for polished and hard-edged containers of stone or stainless steel that complement an overall plan or nearby material; more casual, natural gardens, by contrast, permit choosing a wider variety of vessels, such as a wooden half-barrel or clay pots.

Increasingly, home stores, nurseries, and garden centers offer water garden kits that include a container along with all of the other needed components, such as a fountain, lights, and a pump, making the setup quick and easy. After selecting a kit, all you need do is fill it with water and aquatic plants, plug it in, and enjoy the transformation of your indoor or outdoor living space.

FOUNTAINS

A fountain can be a dramatic inclusion in a formal garden pool, a freestanding sculptural element, or simply may offer a playful, sensual place in the garden for water to bubble over a crop of cobblestones.

Fountains are the most formal and deliberate way to create motion in a water garden. In the right setting, as at the center of a raised garden pool, the symmetrical spray of a fountain often is the majestic and signature feature of an entire landscape.

Along with creating visual impact, fountains also evoke another sensation: sound. Splashing water can mesmerize and help mask other sounds, a benefit especially appreciated in crowded, noisy, urban settings.

Successful fountain features require respect for scale and understanding of how the fountain complements the garden's overall design and style. Various fountains will achieve different effects and purposes. There are many fountain styles, and each has a place: an arching flow from a statue above a formal birdbath, a curved spray pattern in a modern pool, a whimsical wall fountain in a small-space garden, or a gurgling waterspout that mimics a mountain stream.

Choose plants to fit your fountain. Some plants are better suited to moving water; shoreline plants will thrive while some marginals and floaters struggle in the slightest current.

(Above) Pedestal fountains have concealed pumps within their column or base. Always carefully level such fountains when they are installed, mounting them on a firm, masonry base.

(Left) Waterspouts flow from their fixtures into a basin with a delightful and musical sound. The sound of flowing water is effective for masking unwanted noise from nearby roadways.

(Bottom) Visually dramatic, wall fountains are more elaborate than most standing fountains, and they often require greater effort to plan and install. The two-tier fountain shown here is a focal point for this garden's brick retaining wall.

SIMPLE POOLS AND PONDS

The basic difference between pools and ponds—or watercourses and streams, for that matter—is formality of design. On a secondary level, simple pools generally contain less complex systems: pumps, piping, filters, and lighting.

Generally, pools are formal and have strong architectural lines. Pools have a long tradition in European gardens, especially Moorish- and Mediterranean-themed spaces, and can be very effective in gardens with a modern look. Pools tend to be geometric with clearly defined boundaries, and they are edged with manufactured materials, such as concrete, bricks, pavers, and tile. Consider garden pools for formal landscape settings, patios, or courtyards. Place a pool in the center of a design, at the end of a planting bed, or where visual axis lines come together at a corner. Both raised pools and those flush with the ground interrupt an otherwise flat plain, reflect sunlight and shadows, add cooling relief, and create a garden centerpiece. Pools containing a fountain make an especially sensual impact by adding the music of moving water.

Garden ponds, by contrast, mimic nature. A well-designed pond looks as if it always was there, as if a small lake was part of the home. Pond shapes are asymmetrical and curved, with soft or sloping edges. Typically, ponds are finished with natural rock and bordered with moisture-loving plants. Water moves by concealed pumps and pipes, by using a simple splash box, or by the effect of a prevailing breeze rippling the surface. Consider a pond for a natural-style garden, especially one with a woodland or tropical setting. Tuck garden ponds in a corner or a side yard, avoiding placement in the measured center of your landscape space. Ponds are a wonderful addition to slightly hidden areas,

(Above) Water lilies and simple ponds are perfect companions. The still water of such features creates an ideal habitat for lilies. The plants, in turn, produce broad leaves that shade and cool the water. By blocking sunlight, the lilies also limit the growth of algae, improving water quality.

places where garden visitors and wildlife alike can visit. Ponds allow a broader choice among aquatic plants than do pools, since they contain many different environments to suit submersibles, shallow- and deep-depth marginals, floaters, and shoreline plants. They encourage and sustain birds, dragonflies, amphibians, and fish.

Despite their design differences, the basic construction is very similar for pools and ponds. The choice to create a pool or pond depends on your overall garden style and your purpose for adding a water feature to your landscape. In either case, pools or ponds of any size or style require greater commitment and effort to plan and build than, say, a simple wall fountain or self-contained water garden. The results, however, are rewarding and spectacular.

Remember also that a pool or pond can be your first step in a phased installation of a larger water garden. Once established, the pool or pond easily can be expanded to include a stream or watercourse [see Watercourses and Streams, pg. 6] Other expansion options might include adding a fountain or creating an adjoining wetland marsh.

Most garden water features can mimic natural streams and ponds. Use native rock to line the waterway and pond edges. Create overhangs that shadow the pond, and build shoreline planting beds for plants that soften the edge between the nearby garden and the feature. Place aquatic marginal plants at the water's edge.

WATERCOURSES AND STREAMS

A watercourse is to a pool as a stream is to a pond. Watercourses generally are straight and linear, while streams are natural, sinuous, and irregular.

Put another way, watercourses are architectural streams. Like streams, they add moving water to a garden; unlike their natural counterparts, they reflect the materials and construction of the surrounding architecture and garden style. Consider a watercourse in a formal garden, either traditional or modern. Design a watercourse in a straight line with an even width, making square turns, and finish them with manufactured materials such as pavers, tiles, concrete, or brick. The use and quantity of plants in a watercourse depends on your specific design. Placing symmetrical planting containers along the edge of a watercourse can be visually effective.

Streams create movement in a natural setting. An installed stream can mimic nature and provide a playful and sensual feature in your garden. The most successful garden streams imitate nature, even those that flow only a short distance. Their dimension, pace, plants, and edges or banks are based on realistic, natural models. Streams look most natural when they meander through the garden, are edged with natural materials, and include plants along their banks. The stream's size, style, and finish must be considered in terms of the overall size of your yard, your intended effect, and your garden style.

Streams invite colorful pathways and bridges, expanding the enjoyment of both the feature and garden that surround it. Youngsters are fascinated by moving water and aquatic creatures, best seen safely from behind the bridge's railing.

Watercourses and streams are made up of the same elements: a header pool or pond at the top of the feature, the channel itself, and a reservoir pool or pond found at the bottom of the feature. Water moves by concealed means through pipes to the header pool, from a submersible pump located in or near the reservoir pool, which recirculates the water at an appropriate flow rate and volume. Even settings that are relatively flat can accommodate a simple watercourse or stream driven by a recirculating pump.

To keep a stream's natural quality, change the direction of the water flow occasionally, creating small pools and currents that linger in the deeper sections of the bed. Watercourses, on the other hand, are best served by steady flows and consistent water levels. Your choice of a watercourse or stream depends on your garden style. Whichever you choose, streams and watercourses will bring excitement to any garden.

W aterfalls enhance the motion and the mood of a garden, whether in a meandering garden stream or a rushing watercourse.

WATERFALLS

The lip of the fall, called a spill stone, is key to a waterfall's construction and determines its appearance: flat, straight-edged rocks deliver smooth curtains of water; knobby, irregular stones or a rock series cause water to splash chaotically as it falls.

The strength of a waterfall depends primarily on the stream flow rate, which is regulated more by the supply pipe and the recirculating pump's pressure than by the slope of the stream. The pump should generate sufficient volume to replace the water's volume at least twice per hour. Waterfalls require a pump system that delivers a larger volume of water than do pump systems serving simple streams or watercourses.

Whether formal or natural, waterfalls serve both a practical and a playful purpose. Children of all ages love to poke their fingers into the center of a water curtain. Too often, safe opportunities to touch water in the garden are lacking or pose a hazard to young children; small waterfalls in a shallow section create safe opportunities.

Locate recirculating pumps away from the direct impact of falls to reduce the amount of sediment that collects in their inlet filter. Always consider the impact of a waterfall when you are planning for your aquatic plants; moving water may disturb some species, narrowing your choices to plants that like moving water.

(Above) Watercourses are stylized streams bounded by linear sides. Waterfalls and riffles in such watercourses also become design options. Such features match well with contemporary homes that feature clean, straight lines and bold colors.

(Bottom) Include a surprise to reward curious visitors to your garden. Here, a ceramic gargoyle provides a playful central figure in the waterfall's source pool.

DRAMATIC WATER GARDENS

Combining water features—streams with multiple waterfalls, watercourses with several changes of direction, or a pool and fountain—provides spectacular results. Lights, music, structural features, and accessories increase the drama. Plants further showcase your personal style and emphasize your skill and love for gardening.

Begin with lighting. Placed underwater, on the water surface, or concealed among the shoreline plants, lights both highlight the feature and extend its hours of enjoyment into the evening.

Consider an audio system. Hide speakers within plantings to add music or sound effects when entertaining or relaxing.

Varied edging and shoreline materials are another way to add pizzazz to your water garden's look. Besides standard coping stones, consider a gently sloping pebble or sand beach, a wood deck over the water, and bridges or stepping stones to span the feature.

Plants add life, color, and texture to your landscape. Also use plants to add seasonal interest to your garden. Consider massing one plant, whether symmetrically beside a formal water garden or in casual drifts that mimic nature. Another option is to develop a complete ecosystem in your water feature. You might wish to create a tropical jungle effect along the banks of a waterfall and stream: use plants as a ceiling, an understory, on the water, and along the shoreline, just as in nature.

Let your imagination go as you consider the range of water garden designs, options, and aquatic plants that are available.

(Opposite) Every water feature is inherently dramatic. Those that combine elaborate elements, exotic plants, lighting, and other imaginative and eye-catching finishing touches are especially striking. They become the focal point for the entire landscape.

This chapter is a guide to the key elements you need to consider as you refine and formalize your ideas into a comprehensive plan.

First, assess your existing garden site and consider how adding a water garden will impact your landscape. Once you understand your location, you'll want to define the purpose of your water garden, whether for quiet reflection or to add an element of action and sound to the setting. The purpose of your garden dictates many decisions to follow, including the nature of structural features, the size and style of the mechanical devices you will install to make your feature function, and the variety and placement of plants you'll need to complete your garden.

General information is included for the construction of several styles of water gardens: the skills and materials required, the tools and equipment needed, and the sources for plant varieties to enhance and sustain it. You also can discover traditional and new options for gathering information and expert advice about each element of the project. Look for articles in periodicals or on an electronic resource, or talk one-on-one with a Master Gardener at an aquatic nursery. You may even find a book to help you, perhaps right under your nose.

This checklist is useful for every conceivable style of water garden, whether you're creating a natural stream or hanging a formal wall fountain. It helps refine and define your dreams, answers questions about the process, reduces your effort through planning, and conserves your resources. By the end, you'll have a basic understanding of what's needed to create a water garden and be in a perfect position to produce a plan for constructing your project.

All of the steps required to create six water feature projects are presented in this book: self-contained water gardens, garden ponds with preformed liners, garden ponds with flexible liners, simple streams or watercourses, streams with waterfalls, and fountains. Understand and organize all the tasks required to create each of these features by using the project planner at the end of this chapter [see Water Feature Project Planner, pg. 18].

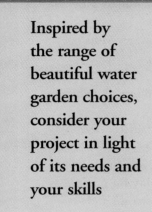

Inspired by the range of beautiful water garden choices, consider your project in light of its needs and your skills

A Garden Checklist

Visit an aquatic nursery early in the planning of your water feature to give you ideas regarding the plants and accessories that eventually will fill your pond, pool, stream, or watercourse. Most of the nurseries have display gardens that demonstrate many of the options and equipment available for your own water feature.

SITE AND PURPOSE

Of the many questions you'll ask as you design, build, plant, and care for your water garden, perhaps the most important are "Where?" and "Why?" The location and purpose of your water garden demand thoughtful consideration. A water garden that's placed in an appropriate location and designed to fulfill your anticipated purpose will deliver lasting enjoyment.

The existing conditions on your site in large part determine the type, size, and placement of your water garden. Determining the location of your water feature often is a process of elimination. Take a fresh look at your yard, reviewing its practical and aesthetic qualities:

- **Regional location**—planning for every climate and USDA plant hardiness zone [see Plant Hardiness Around the World, pg. 115].
- **Home and garden architecture**—fitting your idea with the structures, paths, patios, decks, and other features already existing in your landscape.
- **Underground utilities**—identifying power and water sources.
- **Sun and shade**—meeting aquatic plants' need for 5–6 hours of direct sunlight each day to grow and thrive.
- **Prevailing winds**—tracking both the intensity and direction that affect water flows, surface patterns, and plant needs.

Structural water features, such as the impressive fountain shown here, must be designed to fit the garden site and its conditions.

- **Grade and slope**—gauging general suitability for pools and ponds or stream and watercourses.
- **Property line and setback**—placing water features while maintaining safety for neighboring residents.
- **Existing elements**—retaining or removing trees, features, and existing structures to accommodate the new water feature's design and facilitate its construction.

Finally, consider how your options change the way you'll use your landscape—as a restful retreat, barrier, or center for entertaining. Understanding the purpose of your water garden will help you reach decisions. Seek the reasons behind your preference for a certain type of water feature. They may vary from a desire to explore new plant varieties to a wish for movement and sound in your garden. It is important to articulate and keep in mind your reasons as you design your water garden.

The ultimate goal of a well-designed landscape is to achieve harmony throughout your garden. Design the garden to fit your site and purpose [see pg. opposite] while also keeping the project in the proper scale and scope. The size of your water garden and the scope of your construction project depend on two primary considerations: your site and you.

Scale is the physical size of the garden in relation to the site. Scope is the project's complexity in terms of the number of features, difficulty of installation, and quantity of the resources that it requires. The two issues are closely related: typically, the grander the scale of the feature, the more involved the scope for constructing and installing it. Your planning and skills make a difference in deciding the scale and scope of your project, and in the decision to seek aid and assistance during the installation.

Choosing the scale, in fact, determines the size and scope of your water garden in a way that either makes it the primary focus of your yard or relegates it to a background role. Match a large water feature to a large yard, and a modest, self-contained water feature or fountain to one with a smaller scale.

SCALE AND SCOPE

(Above) Fitting a water feature into an existing landscape begins by matching its scale—size within the context of the site—with the rest of the garden.

Choosing the opposite—even if you have the skills and resources available—will have less than desirable results.

Remember, a tiny garden pond may seem easier to build than a large one, but in fact requires most of the same steps and nearly as much effort to construct. Given that fact, ultimately, a successful water garden is one that fits its site—matches its scale. Choose the right feature for your particular garden and landscape site.

If you find that your building project's scope is too complex, it's better to reconsider some elements and finishes than to reduce the size of the water feature. Think in terms of completing elements in discrete phases spread over a period of time. As long as you plan ahead, the installation of various elements often can occur in phases over a period of months or even years.

(Left) Small-space gardens are appropriate settings for simple water features. In such landscapes, they dominate their surroundings while providing a focal point of great interest.

SKILLS AND MATERIALS

In the past decade or so, creating water gardens has become infinitely easier and simpler by the introduction of prefabricated liners and integrated systems. Before embarking on any project, take time to acquire needed skills of layout, construction, planting, finishing, and caring for water gardens.

Creating a pool or pond by installing a liner is easier than creating one with the traditional method of pouring concrete. Flexible liners mold to the excavated area and create a watertight seal. Rigid, preformed ones fit into precisely excavated holes made to their measurements. You'll still need general masonry and carpentry skills, and you'll also need help for measuring, lifting, and setting the liners in place.

Installing submersible recirculating pumps and filters is straightforward due to integral workings, sealed housings, and simple installation kits. Installing a pump is a snap—actually, a clamp or screw—even for first-timers. It's still helpful to understand basic electrical and plumbing tasks, specifically how to tie into existing systems and connect components. You'll use familar fastening tools and quickly become proficient.

Most finishing materials and accessories are quite easy to install. While some require masonry or carpentry skills, most rely simply on your creativity in choosing a site for the installation and assembling the components.

Planting water gardens is best accomplished with an understanding of aquatic plants and a respect for their placement and care. The most important of these is recognizing the natural environment in which they originally grew.

You'll also need to maintain optimum water quality. Some aquatic plants and helpful bacteria actually regulate the water, though you'll also need to regularly test water. It's easy to use a test kit, reading and following its instructions on a regular maintenance schedule.

Finally, you'll need to periodically clean the feature; repair its liner, pump, and filter; manage your plants and planting containers; and care for filters and other devices necessary to the water feature. For the most part, gentle handling of the varied components is the essential skill involved, although repairs may require gaining familiarity with patching compounds and sealants, piping, and plumbing or becoming familiar with new skills, tools, and materials.

If your water garden is complicated or involves significant grade or utility adjustments, consider consulting a trade professional for their advice or assistance. Regulations in some locales require a professional site evaluation before a building permit can be issued or you may begin any construction. An inspection may be required before use.

(Above) Useful skills for installing a water feature include use of common masonry techniques to set coping stones, lay brick, and mortar rock. These techniques are simple to master, and many home centers hold regular classes that reveal the secrets of working with brick, mortar, and stone.

The components needed to install a water feature include (clockwise from top) rigid plastic liners, flexible PVC liners, sump pumps, submersible pumps, above-water pumps, flexible EPDM liners, and hose.

(Above) Large and small earth moving machines are available from equipment rental yards for those experienced in their use. Consider your skills and whether you should consult with an experienced operator to excavate a large water feature.

TOOLS AND EQUIPMENT

(Below) Tools needed for repairing a water feature include a level, shovel, bucket, patching materials, rubber gloves, and boots.

As you refine your water garden project's scale and scope, and you evaluate your skills for performing the installation of a water feature, make a list of the various tools and equipment you'll need. Some items, such as shovels, trowels, and basic carpentry tools, already may be in your tool shed or garage. Others may be new and unfamiliar, notably those devices used to move, test, and condition water. Be sure to include them in the scope and budget for your project even if you choose to acquire, borrow, or rent them. It's best to rent large, infrequently used tools and equipment for excavation and installation of the feature, and to acquire those used for its care. Equipment rental yards are readily available in most locales and can supply you with the equipment you need. Most can also supply references for operators and installers able to assist you with your project.

Plan on marking the precise shape and dimensions of the feature before you start digging, in a process called layout, using a tape measure, wooden stakes or other marking devices, a string line, and a line level.

A sharp shovel or spade will ease the excavation. You'll also want a dry, straight piece of lumber long enough to span the breadth of any two points within the excavated area to use as a straightedge. It will balance a carpenter's level as you dig, grade, and shape the excavated area. A heavy-duty tarp is useful for piling removed turfgrass and topsoil.

When planning underwater shelves for submerged plants, you'll need carpentry tools to create a plywood or cardboard template that profiles the shelves' shape, depth, and slope in relation to the bottom of the pond; as you excavate, gauge each section for accuracy by fitting the template into place.

You'll need tools to tamp and compact soil, creating a stable base for the liner. Other installation tools include wire and PVC pipe cutters, electrical and plumbing tools, and basic masonry tools such as buckets, mixing tools, and trowels for mortaring and finishing the feature's edges and spillstones. Most aquatic plants can be installed using familiar garden hand tools.

Once your water garden is filled and operating, you'll need an auxilary pump, hose, buckets, and sponges. Good work gloves, sun protection, and some skid-resistant water shoes or hip waders will come in handy when you have to enter the water to care for the plants or repair equipment.

AQUATIC PLANTS

Creating a water garden opens up a new and fascinating range of plants suited for aquatic and moisture-rich environments. Many unique aquatics are featured here [see Encyclopedia of Aquatic Plants, pg. 79]. Whether you use them to enhance the banks of a stream, attract and sustain wildlife, or provide new textures and colors to reflect off your pool's surface, growing plants for water gardens is a rewarding experience.

There are four basic categories of aquatic plants:

(Top right) It's important to place plants in their proper environment within the water feature. Depending on where the plants grow in nature, they may require deep or shallow submersion, running or still water, or planting in boggy soils.

(Bottom) Aquatic nurseries often display plants in settings similar to those you will use in your home water feature. Check care tags for additional information.

Shoreline: Also called bog plants or boggy marginals, shoreline plants grow in the soil outside the watertight liner that forms the water feature. Some require damp, well-drained soil. Others thrive in constantly moist conditions. In a natural environment, shoreline plants receive moisture from their pond. In water gardens, plant them in the same manner as for most garden plants. They require regular waterings to maintain adequate moisture.

Floaters: Plants living with roots that dangle in the water, unanchored in soil, are called floaters. Plants that lay on the surface are called surface floaters, while those that primarily dwell underwater are called submerged oxygenators. Submerged oxygenators serve minor water quality functions by helping to balance the oxygen levels of the water, mitigate algae growth, and provide food for fish and plant life. In a natural environment, floaters sometimes root into the bottom of the pond. In water gardens, they remain unattached or are planted as deep-water submersibles.

Marginals: There are marginals of two types, both grow in submerged soil within the liner. Shallow-depth marginals grow in water less than 6 inches (15 cm) deep, while deep-depth marginals grow in water 6–12 inches (15–30 cm) deep. Many of the shallow-depth marginals also grow in constantly moist shoreline soil. In a natural environment, marginals grow in soil at the bottom of ponds or streams. In water gardens, plant marginals in the soil of a weighted container, cover the soil with gravel, and submerge the container to the required depth. Place the containers on shelves built into preformed liners or on risers at the bottom of a feature. Marginals add height along the perimeter and soften edges of water features.

Deep-water submersibles: Plants rooted deeper than 12 inches (30 cm) underwater are considered deep-water submersibles. They include water lilies and lotus plants. The platelike leaves of water lilies aid water quality by blocking sunlight and provide shelter and shade to aquatic life. In a natural environment, they grow in soil at the bottom of a pond. In a water garden, plant them in containers and sink them to the required depth.

Three convenient sources for information about water gardens and plants are aquatic nurseries (top); periodicals, brochures, books, and catalogs (below); and electronic resources (bottom). Remember, local experience and knowledge is more helpful than that from a more general source found outside your area.

SOURCES AND RESOURCES

Gardening is a passion and a hobby shared by millions of people around the world. If you are new to the ways of water gardening, you'll discover an abundance of knowledge, wisdom, and inspiration is available to you.

As a starting point, take an after-dinner walk through your neighborhood or make a weekend visit to a nearby historic home, a public park, or a botanical garden. You'll likely find a palette of ideas in proper context. Bring your camera and a notepad to record what you see and like; if you feel inquisitive, knock on a few doors or seek out the homeowner, groundskeeper, or docent to learn more. Watch the garden section of your newspaper for tours and clubs in your area dedicated to water gardening.

Visit a nursery that specializes in aquatic plants and ask the staff for advice. A good gardening expert at a nursery, garden center, or home improvement store will spend time helping you narrow your focus and choosing aquatic plants and other materials well suited to your location. Most can direct you to information specific to the most appropriate plants, construction materials, and accessories for your needs, all the while boosting your knowledge base.

Remember your local library has a wealth of information on gardening and construction projects. Cooperative extension services from the United States Department of Agriculture [USDA] and its counterpart at Agriculture Canada also provide reliable information on local soil and the plants that will thrive in your area.

Check electronic resources for information dedicated to water gardens: sites where gardeners share information, post articles, showcase stellar gardens, and offer their expertise [see On-line, pg. 118].

Start a simple file to keep all your inspiration and newly-developed knowledge organized. Include a collection of favorite images from periodicals, photos from gardens you've visited, answers to questions you've jotted down, and nursery or home center brochures and flyers that help you plan for a water garden. The file also might contain a note concerning your garden's purpose, your requirements, your wishes, and key facts you've discovered about your site. This idea file will serve you well. Even after your feet are wet—so to speak—continue to collect information and ideas to expand your water garden knowledge and supplement your own experience.

WATER FEATURE PROJECT PLANNER

Conceptually, there are few limits to the types and styles of water features you may conjure, create, and enjoy. There are a few basic types of projects, however, that you can alter to fit your scale, scope, climate conditions, and personal taste. If your goal is to create a dramatic water garden with many elements, pick and choose from the steps listed for each project when planning its components. To help you plan the most common water feature construction projects, listed here are the specific steps for each of six projects:

SELF-CONTAINED WATER GARDENS

Overview pg. 36
Plan and design pg. 25
Choose and prepare container pg. 37
Apply sealant or install liner pg. 37
Choose plants pg. 79–113
Plant pg. 57
Maintenance and care pg. 67

GARDEN POND WITH PREFORMED LINER

Choose the site pg. 22
Plan and design pg. 25
Select liner pg. 27
Select pump pg. 29
Electrical needs pg. 32
Install utilities pg. 38–40
Layout and excavation pg. 42
Install recirculating pump pg. 43
Install liner pg. 44
Finish pg. 50–51
Choose plants pg. 79–113
Plant pg. 57
Maintenance and care pg. 67

GARDEN POND WITH FLEXIBLE LINER

Choose the site pg. 22
Plan and design pg. 25
Select liner pg. 27
Select pump pg. 29
Electrical needs pg. 32
Install utilities pg. 38–40
Layout and excavation pg. 42
Install recirculating pump pg. 43
Install liner pg. 45
Install lighting pg. 54–55
Finish pg. 50–51
Choose plants pg. 79–113
Plant pg. 57
Maintenance and care pg. 67

STREAM WITH WATERFALL

Choose the site pg. 22
Plan and design pg. 25
Select liner pg. 27
Select pump pg. 29
Electrical needs pg. 32
Install utilities pg. 38–40
Layout and excavation pg. 42
Install recirculating pump pg. 43
Install liner pg. 47
Create waterfall pg. 49
Install lighting pg. 54–55
Finish pg. 50–51
Choose plants pg. 79–113
Plant pg. 57
Maintenance and care pg. 67

SIMPLE STREAM
OR WATERCOURSE

Choose the site pg. 22
Plan and design pg. 25
Select liner pg. 27
Select pump pg. 29
Electrical needs pg. 32
Install utilities pg. 38–40
Layout and excavation pg. 42
Install recirculating pump pg. 43
Install liner pg. 47
Finish pg. 50–51
Choose plants pg. 79–113
Plant pg. 57
Maintenance and care pg. 67

FOUNTAIN

Choose the site pg. 22
Plan and design pg. 25
Select pump pg. 29
Select fountain and fixtures pg. 30–31
Electrical needs pg. 32
Install utilities pg. 38–40
Install recirculating pump pg. 43
Install fountain pg. 52–53
Install lighting pg. 54–55
Choose plants pg. 79–113
Plant pg. 57
Maintenance and care pg. 67

Like many activities, success in water gardening is rooted in good preparation. Good planning is essential to reaping the full rewards of a water feature and adequately nurturing aquatic plants. While it may be motivating to pick up a shovel and start digging out a streambed, knowing how that act fits into the overall project will make your efforts easier, more meaningful, and more successful.

This chapter presents all the steps necessary to design your water garden—whether modest or spectacular. It begins with selecting the exact spot for the feature, helps refine the style and scale of your project, and shows you how to compile your decisions for ready reference onto a garden plan. Once your plan is in place, use it to select liners, pumps, fountains, plants, and the other elements necessary for implementing your design. If you will be adding utility systems for your water feature, use your garden plan to locate the water and electrical lines through your landscape and to the water feature.

Designing Water Gardens

You get many great payoffs from completing a garden plan. Design is often a regulating force. Taking the proper steps before you dig will help you simplify and refine your ideas and will answer many questions before they arise. It's better to document the location of a utility line on paper, for example, than discover it after you're knee deep in an excavation. It is especially important to have a garden plan if you will install your project in phases. With a plan, you can organize your building projects as time and resources allow, while keeping your long-term goals in focus.

A garden plan also hastens permit or regulatory approvals, usually required by building codes in your locale. It's a handy reference if you plan to use professionals—electricians, plumbers, masons, carpenters—to help you with the installation. Take it with you when selecting building materials and supplies to avoid return trips midproject, and use it when discussing plant choices with nursery and garden center staff. Finally, a garden plan assures that your project will harmonize with your existing landscape.

All water features consist of similar components. Even this elaborate pond shares with other water gardens a waterproof liner, recirculating pump system, aquatic plants, and attractive finishing touches.

SELECTING THE SITE

At first glance, it may be obvious where a water garden fits into your landscape. It's always a good idea, however, to confirm a proper location using the following criteria:

Grade: The right grade depends on the type of water feature you're planning. Place ponds or pools on level ground near the highest point in the yard, a place high above the water table and safe from any runoff. Streams or watercourses, by contrast, are best on gentle slopes, either natural or excavated. Adjust the grade of your landscape with terraces and retaining walls; if a low spot is otherwise ideal, plan to build up the site and divert natural drainage away from the feature.

Climate: Place water gardens in areas that receive 5–6 hours of sun a day so aquatic plants can thrive. Plant choices will be limited in shady locations. Shelter them from prevailing wind, which disturbs the water, and locate them away from trees.

Soil: The soil at the site affects shoreline plants and the stability of the liner. Aquatic plants positioned within the water feature are isolated from the existing soil. Shoreline plants, however, require well-drained to constantly moist garden soil. Sample soil at your proposed site to determine its type. Clay soil is dense and slow-draining; it provides a stable base for pond and pool liners. Sandy soil is loose and drains quickly; plan to solidify it before liner installation.

Utilities: Locate all underground utility lines by contacting your provider. Move or adjust the dimensions or site of the water garden rather than moving existing lines.

Access: Mark the outline of your proposed feature with a hose or rope. View it from different angles and distances, and walk around it to make sure there's plenty of space to care for it. Plan on a fence and gates—you'll want to make sure that the feature will be safe for children and pets that might wander into your yard.

Your water feature will become a permanent and eye-catching element in your landscape. Try to envision the finished feature before you begin construction, using stakes and string or other markers to outline the feature on your site. Make adjustments now, when they are easy.

SAFEGUARD CHILDREN

Children love water. Few can resist dabbling or feeling it, kicking and splashing. But for young children, a water garden can be a hazard and caution is advised. Most accidents happen when unsupervised, curious children fall into a pond or pool. Keep garden gates closed and maintain adult supervision whenever a child is in the garden. Remind children to stay a safe distance away from the edge of the water. Fostering a passion for gardening in young children is a rewarding experience; take steps to ensure it is a safe one, as well.

WATER GARDEN ELEMENTS

Most of the elements essential to water gardens are hidden in the finished feature, concealed by necessity and design. They include the liner, its pump and water circulation system, finishing materials, electrical and water supplies, and aquatic plants. The components shown here are found in most water features:

A Liners for ponds, pools, and streams are commonly available in three forms: rigid preformed units (top left), EPDM flexible rubber (right), and PVC plastic (left).

B Pumps are of two types: submersible (left) and above-ground (right). Both types have models in a range of capacities, measured by their flow rate in gallons per hour (liters per hour) and pressure of flow (head height).

C Many finishing materials are appropriate for water gardens, either formal, casual, or natural in style. They include masonry block, brick, flagstone, fieldstone, cobble, and gravel.

D Plan on a GFCI-protected A.C. electrical circuit and a plumbed water supply. The electrical supply powers the recirculating pump and, with a transformer, 12-v. D.C. lights. The water supply is attached to an automatic refill float valve that operates in a manner similar to that of a household toilet, keeping the feature full.

E Aquatic plants complete the garden: choose a selection of floaters; shallow- and deep-depth marginals; deep-water submersibles; and moist-soil shoreline plants.

CONCEPT TO DESIGN

Create a garden plan on graph paper or using a computer software program developed for landscape design. Good design mixes common sense with a few universal rules while recognizing past successes learned through experience: if the concept and vision feel right, they probably are; if you're going with conventional wisdom, the probability of your success increases.

Begin with a base plan to indicate everything that exists on your site now. Start with a copy of your property's survey for an accurate rendering—they're usually available from the local building department—or measure your property and carefully transfer the distances to scaled graph paper. Mark the placement of your home, other permanent structures, and features you plan to retain on the site: existing trees, planting beds, paths, and decks or patios. Mark the location of all underground utility lines. Accurately record the dimensions and locations of these components. Add to this the information you've discovered about your garden: the sun and shade pattern, the wind direction, and any changes of elevation on your site.

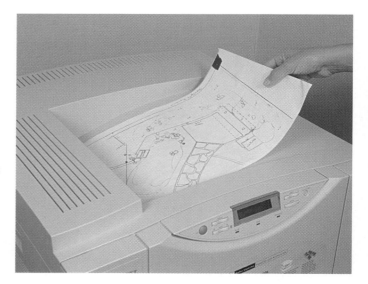

Use a photocopier's enlarging and reducing function to increase the scale of your plans and make details clear. Use computer software design programs to draw clean, clear site plans and detail construction plans, following the software's instructions.

Place an overlay of tissue paper on your base plan, or make several photocopies of it for experimentation. Try different shapes and placements for your water garden. Consider different configurations, sizes, and styles [see Selecting the Site, pg. 22]. Once you're satisfied it meets your needs for use and purpose, transfer the shape, scale, and placement of the feature to a fresh tissue overlay. This will be the master plan for your water feature—use it to prepare details and elevation drawings.

Working on your master plan, use different colored pencils to indicate existing features and structures and those that will be newly built. Show existing and new plants by indicating their planting location with a point, and then drawing a colored circle around the point to indicate their spread when they grow to their mature size.

Date your plan. Record later adjustments in another color. Date the addendum for a clear record of your decisions. Once you're satisfied with your design, make photocopies, using the machine's enlarging function to make detailed drawings at larger scales.

If your project is complex, make separate detail drawings for each construction element. Show elevations—a cutaway profile—of the site, material specifications for utility runs, and construction details.

Remember that most locales require you to comply with regulations, codes, and covenants. Use your plan when applying for building permits and approvals, and when inspectors come to call.

Try out your ideas on paper before you proceed to the garden. Photocopies of your base plan make exploring ideas easy. Use tracing paper overlays to sketch your ideas in colored pencil. After you have decided on a shape, layout, and design, copy your working diagram onto the base plan.

PLANNING AND DESIGNING A WATER GARDEN

The purpose of an accurate, scaled bird's-eye view plan for your water garden is to specify every necessary component. It's your single reference for site placement of elements, choice of building materials and plants, and construction details. It also may be required for permits and inspections. The plan serves as an archive record of your project's specifications after completion. To create your plan on paper, follow these steps:

1 On scaled graph paper, draw the site and its measurements in the general area of the feature. Include existing structures, trees, and all utility lines, plus changes of elevation. This is your base plan.

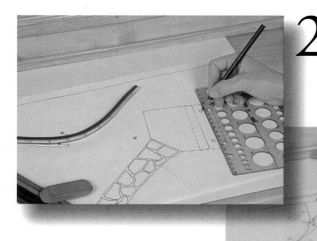

2 On a tissue paper overlay or photocopy, experiment with different options for your feature's location, style, and structure until you're satisfied it meets your criteria.

3 Transfer your final measurements to a clean overlay. Draw electrical supplies and water sources, the path of your recirculating pipe, and the position of the skimmer intake and water discharge.

4 Use colored pencils to mark edge materials and landscape plant choices around the pond. Remember that the pond requires full sun and access. Next, choose aquatic plants and indicate their planting points.

5 Transfer your plant selections to a list for easy reference and for use when you visit your aquatic nursery. Note your plant requirements, including bloom color, season of bloom, variety, selection, and care needs.

WATERPROOF LINER

(Right) Liners—whether rigid and preformed or flexible— underlay nearly all water features. They retain water, of course, but also prevent soil from entering the feature. Lined features usually are bordered by rock and should be layered with gravel, both to disguise the liner and to protect it from sunlight.

(Bottom) Waterproof flexible liners underlay most natural-appearing water gardens. The liners are made of EPDM, a flexible butyl rubber material similar to tire inner tubes. It is easy to lay and trim. With proper installation and protection from sunlight, it usually will last 20 years or more.

The primary purpose of a waterproof liner is to enclose and retain water. It also helps maintain the water's quality. There are two types of liners, flexible and rigid.

Flexible liners are sheets that conform to any water garden's size, shape, or depth. They fold or crease to accommodate curves, marginal shelves, and other contours. They are ideal for large, asymmetrical garden ponds and pools, and especially are well suited for streams and watercourses. The best flexible liners are made from butyl or EPDM rubber. Thinner PVC and polyethylene liners are unsuitable for pond or stream water features. Rigid liners are best for small projects and raised pools.

Liners are available in dark and light colors; darker colors tend to appear more natural, enhance reflection, and allude to greater depth. Protect all liners from the sun's ultraviolet rays to keep them from aging. Water, rock, plants, and edging materials help shield the liner. A liner's topmost section can become exposed if the water level drops from evaporation. The toughest liner materials— rigid fiberglass and flexible butyl rubber— usually can withstand short-term UV exposure without incurring cracks, leaks, or other damage.

SELECTING WATER LINERS

A Rigid pools are made from plastic and more durable fiberglass. Available in a limited number of sizes and shapes, they generally have modest water capacities and appear larger out of the ground than when installed.

P ool liners are available in three common forms: rigid plastic, EPDM flexible rubber, and PVC flexible plastic. Rigid liners, also called molded and preformed liners, are created in a mold with a set shape and have limited flexibility. The best flexible liners are those made of rugged, durable, EPDM rubber—a tire inner-tubelike material. They will last many years and allow you to create complex shapes. PVC liners are inexpensive, easy to puncture, and require replacement before either other type. Bring your garden plan and site measurements, and consider these details when choosing a liner for your water feature:

B The best flexible liners are made of EPDM. Choose liners that will span your feature's length and width, after adding double its maximum depth to each measurement. Avoid joining two liners, if possible, because such points are prone to leaks.

C Select dark colors that create an illusion of depth and enhance reflection. You will cover the entire liner with gravel and boulders to protect it from UV exposure that could cause premature aging.

D Consider combining smaller pools to create larger features, as you would to construct the header and reservoir pools of a stream. Flexible liners appear most natural for home applications, and the preformed liners are quick and easy to install.

RECIRCULATING PUMPS

Pumps circulate the water in your feature. They are reliable and easy to install, adjust, and maintain. Besides powering fountains or streams, pumps circulate water through pipes to submerged filters and skimmers, where it is cleaned and reused, over and over. A pump also comes in handy when it's time to clean the pool or pond. Attach a hose to the pump's cleanout outlet and it will pump out the water.

Most residential water gardens use a submersible, underwater pump. It sits on raised legs or a platform above the bottom to reduce the hazard of sediment and debris clogs. The pump draws water through an intake pipe and a filter screen, which catches debris that could clog and damage motor parts, and pushes it to another location through a pressurized delivery pipe. Surface-mounted pumps, located in concealed enclosures above ground and away from the feature, are more common in water gardens with large streams and multiple elements, or those that cover a large area.

Pumps move water from the reservoir pool to the header pool, lifting it in the process. Most pumps run continuously and are maintenance-free and durable. Choose one based on the volume of water in your feature, allowing for its complete replacement at least twice hourly.

Select a pump based on its capacity, which is measured in gallons per hour [GPH] (liters per hr. [LPH]). Some pumps' flow rates may be listed in gallons per minute [GPM] (liters per min. [LPM]). If your pump will lift water a considerable height, also consider its pressure of flow rate, or head height. Generally, a pump should be able to circulate half of the water volume contained in your feature in an hour's time. Moving water uphill, some distance, or to deliver a broad fountain pattern typically requires pumps with higher GPH (LPH) and pressure ratings.

SELECTING PUMPS FOR WATER FEATURES

Know its purpose before you choose a pump. Some units deliver a high volume at low pressure, best suited for streams; others a low volume at high pressure, better suited for fountains. Understand the purpose and you will be able to pinpoint the correct unit. Pump makers have simplified the process by offering compatible piping and related components. Use only components designed and rated for outdoor and underground use. To choose a pump, follow these steps:

1 Calculate the volume of water in your pond or stream by multiplying its average length, width, and depth. The pump's flow rate in GPH (LPH) should equal or exceed the total pond volume. Even large-volume pumps are of modest size. The pump shown is an above-ground model rated at 1,000 GPH (3,875 LPH).

2 The best choice for most water features is a submersible pump. High-efficiency models are designed to use less power and are most reliable. Choose a pump with raised feet around its intake to reduce the potential for sediment clogs. Plan to install it in a skimmer intake box or mounted on a raised platform.

3 For complex features, or for sites where maintenance access is restricted, choose an above-ground pump. Locate it near a power supply, close to the intake. If needed, enclose it in a weatherproof housing.

4 For fountains, calculate the height and diameter of your desired spray pattern. Check information contained with the spray head assembly, as most fountain packages provide general pump guidelines.

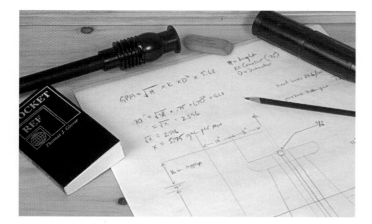

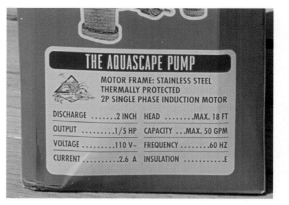

5 Check the information on the housing and package for the pump's electrical requirements, the necessary size and type of piping, and compatibility with accessories.

FOUNTAINS AND WATERSPOUTS

Basically, all fountains operate identically: a concealed recirculating pump designed to deliver a low volume of water at a high pressure is attached to one of the various styles of nozzles or fountainheads, creating the desired effect. Waterspouts—also called bubblers, simple sprays, and splash boxes—have a water reservoir buried underground. The reservoir contains the pump that pushes water through tubing to the waterspout, replicating a natural, bubbling spring.

Fountains either have an integral, dedicated pump or are connected by a delivery pipe to a remote pump fitted with other components. The size of the pump dictates the height and intensity of the spray, so it's important to select the proper-sized pump for your desired pattern. Even so, the flow rate on many pumps can be adjusted within a range, allowing you some control over the fountain's pattern. Generally, keep the height of the spray less than one-half the width of the pool or pond.

Your choice of the fountain or waterspout itself is governed by your imagination and compatibility within your design. Fountains generally are best suited for formal water features such as the center of a pool.

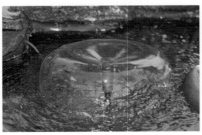

Waterspouts do well in more casual settings. These easily created features are great for close-up contemplative viewing in such locations as a deck, patio, or balcony. They add the sensual qualities of moving water and its burbling, magic music to small-space gardens.

Fountains exist in a host of patterns, from dramatic rotating jets and geysers to tiered domes, rings, bell and tulip shapes, and arching streams; fountains contained within statues or other decorative ornaments add new design elements to your garden. Match the scale of your fountain and its water display to the site you have selected and to the surrounding plants and structures.

Keep other considerations in mind as you choose your fountain or waterspout. If you plan to include fish or plants, avoid fountains constructed with lead fixtures; lead leaches toxins into the water that are a hazard to plants and animals alike. Remember also, while fish can tolerate moving water, some deep-water plants, surface floaters, and oxygenating plants prefer still water with little current. Choose fountains with deep reservoirs if you plan to plant them with aquatic plants; the greater water volume will help keep the quality of the water pure and healthy [see Water Quality and Algae, pg. 70].

A wide choice of spray patterns are available from many garden centers, water garden nurseries, and home improvement stores:

(Left, top to bottom) A spray bubbler, bell, and a two-tier spray.

(Right, top to bottom) One-level Tiffany, two-level Tiffany, and a square pattern.

SELECTING A FOUNTAIN

The width of your fountain's pool should be more than twice the height of the fountainhead to avoid water overspray and wind carried mist. The exposed portions of most fountains are made from reconstituted stone, precast concrete, plastic, or fiberglass, allowing you many options for design, durability, and weight. The hidden, operational components often are included or available separately in kits. Look for these elements, as you select a fountain for your water feature:

2 Pick your fountain basin with the scale of your site in mind. It should include still water areas where aquatic plants may be positioned away from falling water and currents.

1 Choose a fountainhead style, diameter, and spray pattern. For pumps acquired separately, choose a pump rated to deliver water at a flow rate and pressure matching the head fixture. The power cord length should match your site.

3 If you plan to use lighting to provide drama at nighttime, choose a fountain made of a material that will permit drilling holes for wiring. To install a fountain on a deck or other raised surface, choose a model light enough when filled with water to be supported, or construct a masonry base.

4 For in-pond fountains, choose a pump-fountainhead unit with a spray pattern that fits your pond and design.

DESIGNING POWER FOR THE SITE

1 Add the requirements for wattage, voltage, and amperage listed on the label of each device in the system. Reserve 25% extra for future needs.

The size of the pump and the demands of other electrical features determine your overall power needs and whether you need to add a dedicated GFCI-protected circuit or can transform power to 12-volt D.C. form. Confirm specific requirements with your local building department regarding distance between the outlet and the water feature, whether conduit with insulated wire or cable are to be used, and permit requirements. Within the requirements imposed by local codes, follow these steps:

WHAT'S YOUR LOAD?

Add the electrical demands of all the components to determine your total load demand. If your load exceeds 15 amps, you'll need a dedicated, 120-volt alternating current [A.C.] circuit drawn from the main electrical service panel; higher loads may require a 240-volt circuit. Very small demands, however, may be supplied by a low-voltage direct current [D.C.] transformer, which changes alternating current to direct. Install all outdoor outlets with a required ground fault circuit interrupter [GFCI] and insulating ground, which automatically shut off electricity to the entire circuit when the power is interrupted, surges, or short-circuits. Before adding a circuit, always note the overall load demands of your home, which are indicated on the electric service panel.

2 If you need a new circuit, check the service panel for an available breaker slot to service your feature.

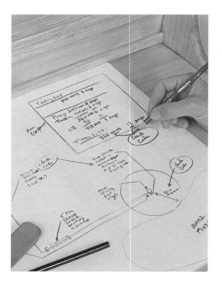

3 If an existing circuit has sufficient capacity, plan the wiring run on paper as an extension, and obtain permits before proceeding, or consult with an electrician if necessary.

4 Note the distance between the source and the feature's outlet, and itemize needed materials: junction boxes, outlets, conduit and wire or cable, stripping tools, and a multimeter tester.

Properly finishing a water garden is an important aspect of its construction and is essential to its overall appearance and enjoyment. Plan all your finishes and garden additions in advance, including edging materials and accessories, so that their needs can be accommodated during construction. All additions should serve your garden's purpose and be selected to suit your garden style.

How the water feature is edged affects its function and beauty. Your selection of edging materials is an opportunity to showcase your personal creativity. As a practical matter, edging materials cover the edge of the liner, mask the line around the feature's perimeter and the surrounding soil, and protect the liner from the sun's UV exposure. Aesthetically, the material choice can make edges clear and distinct—usually best suited for a formal garden—or help blend and obscure the line to create a more natural appearance. Edging materials include coping stones, boulders, ceramic tile, sandy beaches, turf-grass borders, and pebble shorelines. Consider combining several different materials and textures, providing both visual interest and a range of surfaces for plants and wildlife, extending the enjoyment of the garden and providing access to the water.

Accessories include large and small touches that make your garden fit your needs. Large construction projects such as decks and patios often are combined with water gardens, but many water feature accessories are smaller projects. To gain access to your garden and pond, consider a bridge or a series of boulders that double as stepping stones peeking out from the water. If your garden is to be a place of quiet reflection, install benches or other seating nearby. Artwork—from fountains, statues, and viewing balls to original sculptures—adds personality to your water garden. Carefully placed urns, containers, planters, and other elements add both visual interest to the feature and increase the landscape plants that you can use.

FINISHES AND GARDEN ADDITIONS

Surface lighting (left) and submerged fixtures (right) both are wired to a low-voltage D.C. transformer. Using direct current avoids hazard of shock and allows easy installation using simple tools.

T his chapter presents hands-on instruction for building the structural features of your water garden, from simple, freestanding, self-contained gardens to sophisticated waterfalls with lights, from installing a watertight streambed to staging a fountain, and each step in between. It includes easy to follow, step-by-step instructions for bringing utilities to the site and installing both rigid and flexible liners. Assembling pumps and fountains is included, along with methods for finishing the edge of the feature so that it provides safe and secure access while blending nicely into the garden.

After planning and designing, it's time to put your ideas and plans into action and start building your water garden

Depending on your skills and comfort with such activities as excavation, basic carpentry, plumbing, and electrical systems, you may pick and choose which segments of your water garden construction you'll personally perform. If you decide to seek expert help or a tradesperson for some aspects of your installation, you'll still find this chapter helpful as a guide to what occurs and why. Understanding the entire construction process allows you to properly articulate your plans and expectations and inspect the work as it is completed.

Installation and Construction

For the most part, the tasks outlined here apply to all water gardens, regardless of size or style: bring utilities to the site, lay out the feature and excavate, install pumps and liners, and add finishing touches and accents. Depending on the complexity of your design, you might establish streambeds and install waterfalls, fountains, and lights. To gain an understanding of all the tasks involved and to establish your construction schedule, review the project planner that best relates to your design [see Water Feature Project Planner, pg. 18–19]. Check the instructions for each step to determine the skills, tools, and equipment needed. For a basic understanding of these tasks, consider creating a self-contained water garden—it's an excellent first project.

Placing low-voltage lighting within and around a water feature signals the last stage of construction. Finishing touches also include installing coping stones, adding benches and bridges, and planting the shoreline margins.

SELF-CONTAINED WATER GARDENS

The sound of rushing water has been a source of relaxation for centuries. Experiment with a self-contained water garden before moving to create a full-size water feature. Creating a custom garden takes only a few hours to complete.

A wonderful, and wonderfully easy, project for adding a water feature to your home is creating a self-contained water garden. They're popular for use indoors and out. Styles and vessels range from the traditional half barrel to modern sculptures. Both manufacturers and individual artisans offer complete kits with pumps, fountains, and sculptures—you merely fill them with water and plants, and plug them in. If you are purchasing a kit and plan to locate it outdoors, be sure that its pump and wiring is rated for outdoor use.

As with larger water gardens, the water container must be made watertight. Choose a vessel that is structurally sound, clean, and lined with a waterproof coating or a brush-applied waterproofing sealant before you fill it with water and plants. To do it yourself, apply latex sealant with a paintbrush; it's available from most paint suppliers, home improvement centers, and hardware stores.

Once filled, a self-contained water garden is quite heavy. Keep this weight in mind, as well as climate and sun factors, as you locate your garden. Its placement may be limited to areas structurally able to take the load. Use extra caution when placing the water garden on decks and balconies, choosing only those sturdy enough to carry the weight. If in doubt, consult an engineer.

The pumps, fountains, and lights are the same as those used in larger water gardens, although often smaller in size, output, or capacity. Check equipment packaging to determine its electrical requirement. Locate the container near a 110-volt GFCI-protected outlet, even if the water garden requires only a low-voltage D.C. current to operate. Such current is often found on a porch, deck, or patio, or is easily added using a plug-in transformer. If unsure, consult with a licensed electrician before you connect your water garden.

Adding motion, such as a bubbling fountain, gives your self-contained water garden an extra dimension to enjoy. Remember that too much turbulence can affect plant growth; work with your garden center or nursery staff to select plants suited to life near a fountain.

Aquatic plants as a rule require less daily care than do most in-soil container plants, and their care needs generally are simple. Always maintain an adequate water level and good water quality to ensure that your plants have a healthy growing environment.

CREATING A SELF-CONTAINED WATER GARDEN

Producing a freestanding water garden is a great first-time building project and a wonderful family activity. Your garden center or home improvement store should carry all the componets along with sealant, which you brush like paint onto the interior surface of the container. To get your feet wet in water garden building, without actually having to get your feet wet, follow these steps:

1 Select a wear-resistant, ceramic container. Wash and seal its inside surface or install a watertight liner.

2 Drill a hole on the container's side near its bottom. Fit a valve and outlet into the hole, sealing it with aquarium-grade silicon sealant.

3 Fill the container base with 4 in. (10 cm) of rinsed pea gravel. Set a riser on the base and place the pump and filter assembly on it.

4 Arrange risers for plants and install the fountainhead. Connect the fountain to the pump.

5 Rinse, then fill the container with water, checking for leaks. Plug in the pump, and adjust its flow rate.

6 Allow several days for harsh municipal water chemicals to dissipate, then install plants.

WATER AND ELECTRICAL SUPPLIES

Most water features need a dedicated water and nearby electrical supply. Bringing a water line to the site makes maintaining water levels automatic and eases refilling the garden after a cleaning. To power the pump and other electrical equipment, you'll also need power at the site.

Your first priority when bringing water or electricity to your site is to verify the code requirements with your local building department. The scope of your project may require a permit before you begin, as well as periodic inspections during the process.

You'll make underground connections from the source—a water main or manifold—to a dedicated hose bib or water supply connection near the garden; you also may want to install an automatic refill float valve that replaces the water whenever the level drops. To prevent overfilling due to precipitation or a stuck valve, consider installing an overflow valve and a drain pipe bypass extension from the feature, which allows you to pump excess water and drain the feature during maintenance.

For electrical needs, confirm your power requirements and create a plan for running wire from your electric panel or a previously existing outlet to the site [see Designing Power for the Site, pg. 32]. Bury wires in an underground trench. If the trench is less than 18 inches (45 cm) deep, run separate conductor and grounding wires inside rigid metal or PVC conduit. For deeper trenches, run direct burial cable using conduit protection only where the cable descends into or emerges from the ground. Connect the run to an above-grade junction box near the feature. The GFCI-protected outlet should be housed in a weatherproof box at least 12 inches (30 cm) above grade and 30 inches (75 cm) or more from the feature. Before filling the trench, place flat stones to protect the buried conduit or cable against subsequent excavation or garden digging.

To enhance the convenience, safety, and care of your water garden, consider installing options such as above-ground shut-off or flow-controlling valves for easier access to the water system; a switch or automatic timer that controls low-voltage lighting or fountains; and a three-way switch box rather than a single outlet, to accommodate all of your future system expansion.

Install a GFCI receptacle to power your water feature, and regularly test it. Protection against shock hazard and short circuit is built into the outlet, breaking the circuit if either should occur. Test the GFCI monthly to assure safe operation.

An automatic refill float valve senses the water level of your garden's system, adding more water when it falls too low. Usually, the float valve is installed in the skimmer box, as shown here. By mounting it adjacent to the pump, it protects the pump from running out of water and overheating. Because most water features operate 24 hours per day, automatic refill is essential to safe operation.

INSTALLING A WATER SUPPLY TO THE FEATURE

Water supplies using rigid PVC pipe carry water from the household side of the water meter to the feature, where it terminates in a hose bib. An automatic refill float valve attached to the water supply automatically adds water to the feature if its level should drop. Locate all underground utilities before digging, and comply with local code requirements. To install a dedicated water line, follow these steps:

2 Trench from the water supply to the feature, using a machine available at local rental yards.

3 Lay 1-in. (25-mm) schedule 40 PVC pipe in the trench, joining sections with 2-part PVC primer and cement and ell and tee fittings.

1 Turn off the water at the household main. Cut the line and attach a compression tee, a gate valve, and an antisiphon backflow preventer to keep pond water from siphoning into your drinking supply.

4 If a nearby irrigation supply line already exists, cut it and add a lateral extension to lead to the future site of your water feature.

6 Check the entire length of the line for leaks before backfilling the trench with soil from the excavation. Tamp and settle the soil before planting.

5 Install two risers at the extension line's end. To one, attach a hose bib. To the other attach a gate valve that will be connected later to the feature's float valve assembly. Turn on the water and flush the line of debris.

INSTALLING AN ELECTRICAL SUPPLY TO THE SITE

Determine electrical needs and your design before beginning [see Designing Power for the Site, pg. 32]. Follow local codes and obtain permits before proceeding. Use only materials rated for outdoor, underground use. Creatively conceal the outlets and junction boxes, yet make them easily accessible for maintenance. To supply electricity to a water feature's site, follow these steps:

Warning

Shock hazard can cause fatal injury. Always use caution whenever you work with electricity.

2 Install a utility post set in concrete at the site, at least 30 in. (75 cm) from the water edge and at least 16 in. (40 cm) above finish grade.

1 Excavate a trench 6 in. (15 cm) wide of required depth between the point where the run will join the supply panel and the water feature's remote junction box. Lay direct-burial cable or wire in conduit between the two points.

3 Stub up the conduit with a sweep ell connector to a point 6 in. (15 cm) below grade. Extend the wires and rigid conduit to connect to the junction box 12 in. (30 cm) above the finish grade.

4 Turn off power at the main. Add a circuit for your feature at the service panel. Extend and fasten wire from the panel to the junction with cable or conduit.

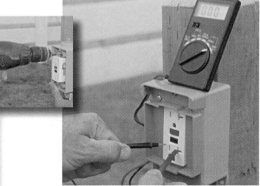

5 Connect black and white wires of the circuit to a GFCI-protected outlet at the remote junction box, then attach the grounding wire to the outlet.

6 Restore power and use a multimeter tester to measure the strength, consistency, and voltage of the current, ensuring proper and safe installation.

Lasting pump operation depends on protecting the pump and its accessories from harm while keeping them accessible for routine maintenance and adjustment. Whether you're using a rigid or flexible liner, the excavated area must be properly prepared to receive, house, and protect it.

PUMP SIZING

Pumps are rated in gallons per hour [GPH] (liters per hr. [LPH]) at a rise of 1 ft. (30 cm) between the pump and its outlet. As actual rise increases, the pump's capacity decreases, slowing the flow rate of the water. Choose a pump that will provide a complete change of the feature's water every two hours.

Calculate the volume and head height of your water feature by multiplying its width, length, and average depth to estimate volume and measuring the rise from pump intake to the discharge outlet to obtain head height. This chart assumes a total water volume of 600 gallons (2,268 l).

Head Height	Pump Required
1 ft. (30 cm)	300 GPH (1,150 LPH)
3 ft. (90 cm)	450 GPH (1,750 LPH)
6 ft. (1.8 m)	600 GPH (2,250 LPH)
8 ft. (2.4 m)	800 GPH (3,000 LPH)
10 ft. (3 m)	1,200 GPH (4,500 LPH)

Pumps: Place submersible pumps and other accessories above the liner to keep the unit free of debris and protect the liner; padded concrete blocks make an excellent, stable, elevated pump base. House above-ground pumps in a weatherproof box to protect them from the elements. Bury delivery pipes from the pump to the header pool or outlet to hide as well as protect them. In cold-winter climates, install a drain valve at the system's lowest point.

Accessories: Choose accessories compatible with pumps and pipe to ease installation and ensure proper operation. Pump accessories include its filters, both those integral to the pump and any stand-alone filters; an automatic refill float valve to maintain water level; a check valve, which prevents backflow of water flow through the pump; and a skimmer to act as a supplemental filter and remove floating debris.

Rigid liners: Excavate a hole that's level and matches the liner's contours. Level it so the water will be uniform and equipment will operate properly. Support all contours of the rigid liner—the rim, bottom, and any marginal shelves—to keep the weight of the water from cracking the liner and causing leaks. Install stable underlayment, then use topsoil removed during excavation to backfill under the liner. If your soil is loose, mix three parts soil with one part cement to stabilize the liner at the rim.

Flexible liners: Sheets of flexible liner material mold to most excavated area's contours. Remove rocks or debris that might puncture the liner under the water's weight. Underlayment further protects and cushions the liner. As the liner first fills with water, smooth out wrinkles and folds; if sections must be joined, overlap them at least 18 in. (45 cm) using compatible self-sealing tape to secure the joint.

The first filling of your water feature allows you to test its pump and water recirculating system. Frequently, sediment and debris also accumulate in the reservoir pool. Pump out the water to remove the sediment. This step will avoid burdening your filter with debris or coating the bottom of the feature with silt and debris.

POND LAYOUT AND EXCAVATION

Mark the dimensions of your flexible-liner pond or stream from your garden plan, including its overall depth and the placement and size of marginal shelves. For rigid liners, trace the outline of the liner and its interior shelves onto the soil. Use a length of hose, flour, or spray paint to mark the outline. To lay out and excavate a pond or stream, follow these steps:

1 Outline the shape of the pond or stream. Place symmetrical rigid liners upside down to mark their shape; place irregular shaped liners upright and outline using stakes. Follow your plan's design dimensions for flexible liners.

2 Use stakes and a line level to establish a level above the excavation. Excavate the entire site to the shallowest shelf, mark again, then dig deeper sections.

3 Use a straightedge and carpenter's level to check that the edges, shelves, and bottom are level.

4 Line the base, sides, and shelves of the hole with special landscape root-barrier fabric.

5 Backfill the excavation with a 4-in. (10-cm) layer of builder's sand. Rake smooth, level to the reference string, and check that correct depth has been met at every point. Add or remove sand as needed.

INSTALLING A RECIRCULATING PUMP SYSTEM

Locate submersible pumps in a skimmer box or within the feature, near the intake point. Place above-ground pumps within 5 ft. (1.5 m) of their intake. Bury all recirculating pipe, keeping it easily accessible, and attach a check valve to prevent siphoning. To install a submersible pump, follow these steps:

2 Use a two-part PVC primer and solvent to cement all junctions of pipe in the recirculating loop.

1 Locate a skimmer or intake box at the the pool's edge and opposite the point of water's entry into the pool. Excavate a shallow trench for the recirculating pipe, extending it from the skimmer to the pump, then to the discharge.

3 Install an O-ring compression fitting to the skimmer or intake box and to the outflow box or discarge pipe. Use the appropriate adhesives, fastening materials, and fittings recommended by the equipment manufacturer.

4 Position, mark, excavate, install, and level the skimmer or intake box. Skimmer intakes should be positioned with their top edge 1–3 in. (25–75 mm) above the future water level.

5 Attach the check valve to the pump, place the pump into the skimmer box, and join the outflow hose to the recirculating pipe leading to the discharge at the header pool or waterfall.

INSTALLING A RIGID PREFORMED LINER

The secret of installing a preformed liner is excavating to the correct shape, dimensions, and various depths and slopes to match its exact dimensions. Finish the excavation and place the underlayment of sand [see Pond Layout and Excavation, pg. 42]. To complete the installation, follow these steps:

1 Gently set the liner in place, making sure its bottom and shelves are set evenly and the liner's lip is flush with the level excavated area.

2 Check level across the length and breadth of the liner. To adjust, press down firmly in slightly high points, or add and remove sand as required.

3 Fill around the liner's sides and rim. Avoid disturbing the liner's position and level. If the feature is large, use a long straightedge to span the feature's sides.

4 Compact the margins alongside the liner, using a tamping tool. Maintain an even level along the perimeter.

5 Add water to the liner. Use a sump pump to remove any sediment. Install a submersible recirculating pump. If desired, add a fountainhead.

6 Trial fit your coping stones or other edging materials to cover the liner. They will protect it from UV-rich sunlight.

INSTALLING A FLEXIBLE LINER

1 In the prepared excavation filled with a layer of sand, stretch underlayment fabric. Overlap seams at least 18 in. (45 cm). Smooth folds and wrinkles.

Installing a flexible liner is simple once the excavation is completed [see Pond Layout and Excavation, pg. 42]. Flexible liners mold to the exact shape of the hole. You'll need helpers to hold the edges of the liner while you position and anchor it. To install a flexible liner, follow these steps:

2 Stretch flexible liner over the underlayment, smoothing any folds or wrinkles. Cover the entire area, avoiding making seams.

3 Weight the liner edges with stones to hold it in position as you smooth the liner and fit it into the excavated shelves and bottom. Trim the liner, leaving a margin 2 ft. (60 cm) wide.

4 Fit the liner to the skimmer and header boxes, using aquarium-grade silicon sealant on all joints and fastening parts with non-corrosive fasteners to avoid leaks.

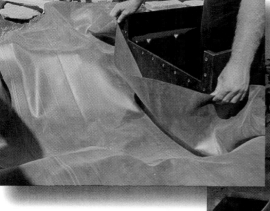

5 Fill the fitted liner with washed gravel, cobble, and boulders to protect it from puncture hazard and exposure to UV-rich sunlight that could cause premature aging of the liner fabric.

ADVANCED WATERCOURSES

Anyone who's hiked in the wilderness most likely has had the pleasant experience of coming across a natural spring welling up from the ground. You can achieve a similar natural effect by building a stream in your garden, or you can create a point of architectural interest in a more formal landscape by installing a watercourse. If you choose to expand the stream or watercourse to include changes in elevation, you also can add the sound and sight of falling water.

All streams and watercourses should be appropriately scaled to the rest of your garden. They are most effective when their design is in keeping with the overall style of the surrounding landscape and your home. Generally, traditional settings are best suited to streams, while modern settings are compatible with watercourses. While stylistically different, the basic components of streams and watercourses are the same. Both have a header pool at their top that begins the water feature, and a reservoir pool or basin at their bottom end that also contains the pump.

Ideas for more complex designs to create a unique water feature include intermediate pools placed along the course, changes in elevation and direction, and bubbling fountains. There's also ample opportunity to add shoreline rocks and plants.

The slope of the stream from the header to the reservoir—top to bottom—should be about a 3% grade, as determined by the rise—height difference—and run—distance—between the header and reservoir pools. Avoid stagnating the flow with a too-shallow grade, or creating uncontrollable torrents with one that is too steep. Rely on the pump's capacity to control the volume of water flow. Remember that abrupt changes of elevation—cascades and waterfalls—are independently planned separate from the stream's grade [see Cascades and Waterfalls, pg. 48]. Line the header and reservoir pools with either rigid or flexible liners and the watercourse channel itself with flexible liner material. If your goal is a natural appearance, remember that creeks in nature flow into deep pools that gradually shallow above the next riffle or cascade.

Streams and watercourses require a steady, full flow of water facilitated by a recirculating pump. The required size, or capacity, of the pump is determined more by the water volume of the reservoir and header pools and less by how fast you want the water to flow [see Pump Sizing, pg. 41].

Seamlessly blending your entire garden landscape into the water feature may take a season or more. Choose perennial plants well-adapted to your climate and suitable for carefree maintenance. Allow them freedom the first season to grow into the site.

LINING A STREAM

1 Trial set all waterfall spill and foundation stones before finalizing your excavation. Check the relative elevation of all spill stones, allowing 4 ¼ in. (11 cm) extra depth for the sand base and the stream liner's thickness.

Line streams in the same manner as pools and ponds. Excavate and line the header and resevoir pools, and excavate for the stream [see Pond Layout and Excavation, pg. 42]. Set any waterfalls [see Creating Waterfalls, pg. 49]. Long watercourses may require overlapping and sealing liner segments with double-sided EPDM adhesive joint tape made for the purpose. To connect the stream and pools, follow these steps:

2 Stretch the liner into position and recheck spill stone elevations. Fasten the liner to the header or filter, using aquarium-grade silcon sealant and corrosion-proof fasteners.

3 Overlap all liner joints 18 in. (45 cm) at a site beneath a spill stone. Lay the lower-stream liner under the upper-stream section, so that its top end is positioned above the final water level of the lower-stream section. Seal all of the joints with EPDM joint tape, then mortar or foam the spill stones atop the liner.

4 Fill the stream liner with gravel and boulders to protect the liner from puncture hazard and exposure to UV-rich sunlight that could cause premature aging of the liner fabric.

5 Flush the stream with water, using a sump pump to remove water and sediment until it is clear. Cleaning the stream prevents sediment and debris from reaching the reservoir pool and clogging the pump and filter.

CASCADES AND WATERFALLS

There's intriguing sensual value in water gardens with audible qualities. Creating a cascade or waterfall adds movement and sound to a water garden. There are numerous ways to achieve falling water effects in your watercourse.

Each cascade or waterfall requires an abrupt change in elevation that interrupts the flowing stream or watercourse. Generally, a fall of about 6 inches (15 cm) will deliver the optimum look and sound. Plan on a deep receiving pool beneath each waterfall, then a slowly rising streambed as the flow approaches the next waterfall.

A foundation stone sits at the point of the elevation change with a spill stone atop it. The spill stone's placement is very important, both vertically and in orientation to level. It should extend over the edge of the foundation stone, so that the water can fall freely into the stream or pool below. It should be placed to partially dam or slow the stream, building a head of water behind.

(Top) Plan planting sites within the margin of the water feature, as was used here as the location for a fern.

(Bottom) Protect still-water plants from fast-moving currents by constructing a deep pool beneath waterfalls, then filtering the water through rock before it enters the main pool.

The spill stone's design regulates the way the water falls. Gate stones set to each side channel the water toward the stone's center and block flow around its edges. In a cascade, the water runs in a smooth curtain over a flat sill from one level to another. In a waterfall, the water splashes down over a rugged rock formation. The width of the spill stone—and how water is channeled to it—helps to determine the appearance and intensity of the falls. Both smooth and splashing waterfall styles are common in nature and are appropriate for either a stream or a watercourse, depending on your desired effect.

A stream with a cascade or waterfall requires a recirculating pump and delivery pipe specifically designed to deliver a high volume of water. The greater the elevation change from the header pool to the reservoir pool, the stronger the pump required [see Pump Sizing, pg. 41]. Choose your pump with excess capacity to create streams and watercourses with rushing water that flows in a torrent.

Creating cascades and waterfalls requires planning prior to excavation. Study creeks and streams in your area to gain an understanding of how naturally occurring streams flow. Especially look at points where water falls. Observing wild streams will help you create a water feature that closely resembles nature.

CREATING WATERFALLS

1 If a liner seam joint is necessary, overlap it 18 in. (45 cm), with the upstream liner above that of the lower stream section and positioning the seam under the future waterfall. Apply double-sided EPDM joint tape between the two liner sections to create a waterproof seal.

W hen natural streams change elevation, they flow from deep pools to gradual shallows, then spill over into a lower pool. In a water feature, install foundation and spill stones to mimic this effect. The stones form a shallow basin behind the waterfall, retaining water in the stream even if the pump is turned off. The spill stone's width, contour and placement determine how the water will fall. To create a waterfall, follow these steps:

2 Position the foundation stones until exactly level within an excavated, Z-shaped shelf atop the liner. Use mortar or waterproof expanding urethane foam to hold them in place.

3 Apply mortar or foam to the foundation stones, then bed the spill stone in place. Check that it's level and its height is below the stream's liner edge.

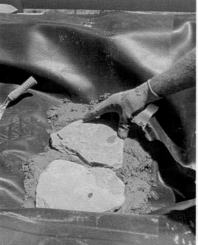

4 Use mortar or foam to install gate stones to either side of the spill stone that rise above the liner edge and direct water to the center of the stream. Disguise the mortar or foam with decorative cobblestones bedded in place.

5 Fill the streambed with gravel and cobblestones above and below the waterfall to hold and protect the liner. Gravel helps the natural-stream effect.

6 Consider installing prebuilt waterfall units as part of your stream. They contain biologic filters of lava rock and are disguised by surrounding stone.

FINISHING TOUCHES

Well-conceived and well-executed finishing touches are essential to a successful water garden project. There are several ways to add just the right finishing touches to your water garden, including edging with various materials, adding structures, or creating accents.

Any finishing touch must be consistent with the style you've chosen for your water garden. Look back to your idea file and remember the purpose of your garden when making your final choices. For a formal design, bricks, geometric stones, tile, and square-finished deck platforms make attractive edgings for a pool or watercourse. Modern sculpture also may help complete the look, depending on your garden's scale and design. For more natural ponds and streams, finishes should look more rugged and random, as if placed there by natural forces. Boulders set into the banks of a stream or pond, even doubling as stepping stones to cross the feature, will look more natural than would square, concrete pavers; a pebble beach or sloping sand-and-turf approach to the water's edge also serves to imitate nature. A rough-sawn deck or handmade bridge will look at home, too—especially if it is consistent in style and materials to structures nearby, such as a gazebo, shed, barn, or your home.

The most prominent finishing touch for a water feature is its edging material. The edging material you choose must be installed correctly so as to assure safety while enhancing the entire water garden. Edgings for formal projects often demand precision and symmetry in design and construction. Even slight variations in a brick or manufactured stone edge's level, spacing, or dimensioning become noticeable. Although a flaw or two might pass inspection when edging a natural-style water feature with coping stones, it's still important that the shape and placement of materials achieve their desired effect and stay firmly in place.

While your edging materials primarily serve aesthetic functions, they also conceal the edge of a liner, hide a pump cable, camouflage light fixtures, keep surrounding soil and water from entering the feature, and protect the liner from UV-rich sunlight damage. Edging materials also serve a valuable safety function, clearly marking the edge and perhaps even barring access to hazardous areas of a water feature. This is an especially important consideration for those with young children or visitors.

A natural wood bench provides a restful site to sit while contemplating the water, adding a practical finishing touch. Here, a heron sculpture adds to the appeal of the setting.

INSTALLING COPING STONES

Coping refers to any material atop a vertical structure, such as the walls of a water feature. Coping stones are a common edging around pools and also are appropriate for traditional ponds and streams. Set the stones flat or to slope slightly away from the water. They overhang the water's edge, to help conceal the liner and provide both shade and protection for fish and amphibians. To install coping stones, follow these steps:

1 Trial set stones atop the liner, resting them on a excavated shelf 1–2 in. (25–50 mm) above the future water level. Use a carpenter's level: they should slope a quarter to half a bubble away from the pond to prevent surface water from flowing into it.

2 Working in small sections, remove each stone, create a bed of mortar, moisten the stone, and loosely seat it into the mortar bed.

3 Position the stones to overhang the edge 2–3 in. (50–75 mm). Check the stones' level to the perimeter and their slope away from the pool. Tap them firmly into place in the mortar using a rubber mallet.

4 Fit stones around skimmer boxes, filters, and other fixtures last. Check that utility covers will fit over the stones prior to mortaring them in place, and avoid mortaring over pipe fittings and electrical connections.

5 Use a damp sponge and water to remove any spills of mortar. Also remove any excess mortar from the pond.

6 Allow the mortar to set for 24 hours. Fill the pond or stream, using a pump to extract water contaminated with mortar.

FOUNTAINS

Every fountain, regardless of style or location, needs a reservoir of water and a recirculating pump to push the water through a delivery pipe to feed a spout or spray head. The shape of the spout determines the pattern assumed by the water. The desired height and diameter of the spray pattern determine the size of the pump. For example, a 300 GPH (1,150 LPH) pump will provide a simple fountain with a spray 2 feet (60 cm) high and 28 inches (70 cm) in diameter. A 1,200 GPH (4,500 LPH) pump will power the same fountainhead to cascade 8 feet (2.4 m) high and spray 128 inches (3.2 m) in diameter!

Above-ground fountains rest on a secure, level base of the proper height. Usually they are constructed from concrete or mortared brick. The fountain's structure conceals the delivery pipe hidden within its column, often including the recirculating pump and electrical cord. For waterspouts, the delivery pipe can be hidden by stones or other facets of the design, or built into paving or walls near the fountain.

Like other structural features, fountains and waterspouts require periodic maintenance. In cold-winter climates, keep the fountainhead and pump submerged in a bucket of clean, cool water in a heated garage or toolshed to prevent its seals and gaskets from drying out and cracking; similarly, treat a concrete or stone statue with a waterproof coating to prevent moisture infiltration that, if it should freeze, could cause cracks.

WALL FOUNTAINS

Wall fountains are distinctive, lively additions that dress up a blank garden wall. Garden centers and nurseries offer a variety of complete wall fountain kits or individual components that allow you to assemble a personalized feature. Aesthetically, most consist of the spout, which often is a sculpted feature secured to the wall, and a base pool or basin. Some have a secondary basin, also attached to the wall between the spout and the pool. This collects water and allows it to overflow into the pool below. A wall fountain is a small version of any feature: its base pool contains water and a submerged, recirculating pump. The pump pushes the water through a delivery pipe and up to the spout on the wall. Wall fountains require electric power for the pump. If you're constructing a new wall, install the delivery pipe and electrical power cable within the wall itself. If you're adding a wall fountain to an existing wall, plan to conceal the pipe and power line behind climbing plants, a containerized tree, artwork, or a trellis.

Large fountains are especially appealing in quiet, tranquil gardens that include changing levels or wooded margins.

INSTALLING A FOUNTAIN

Fountains with self-contained reservoirs and pumps are easy to install and require a minimum of skills. They make an ideal feature for your landscape garden. Locate your fountain near an existing GFCI-protected outlet or install one at the site [see Installing an Electrical Supply to the Site, pg. 40]. To install most self-contained fountains, follow these steps:

1 Measure the base dimension of the fountain and excavate a footing below the frost line, using a concrete forming tube. Fill the form with concrete, strike off, and level the surface with a trowel.

2 Dig a chase or trench for the pump cord from the footing to a GFCI-protected, weatherproof electrical outlet.

3 Install the fountain base on the footing, using flexible adhesive to adhere it to the concrete. Level the base, using stone shims as needed.

6 Fill in all trenches, and mulch the area or install ground cover around the fountain.

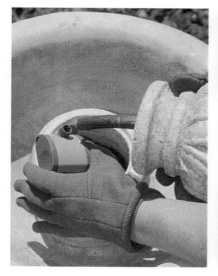

4 Attach the reservoir to its pedestal using flexible adhesive. Install tubing to the fountain pump and fountainhead with its spray nozzle.

5 Fill the fountain with water, checking for leaks, and plug in the pump.

LIGHTING SYSTEMS

A well-designed lighting system remains concealed during the day and reveals itself only at night, extending your hours of water garden enjoyment.

A transformer and special sealed underwater lights are required for water garden lighting. A variety of options exist to alter intensity and color or to control the display. Place lighting fixtures under the surface of the water, highlighting submerged foliage, fish, rocks, and other features. The water surface will reflect the surrounding garden. Consider uplights placed in submerged planting containers, spotlights behind waterfalls to show the movement, and light fixtures attached to fountains.

A 12-volt D.C. system is usually used, run from a transformer attached to a GFCI-protected outlet. Some new pond lights are powered by solar or photovoltaic (PV) cells and storage batteries, though such devices are larger than regular lighting fixtures.

Remember to use traditional garden lighting around your water feature, too. It helps blend the feature into your existing landscape. Position uplights beneath your trees, shrubs, and streamside grasses, to gently accentuate branches and foliage, reflecting them on the moving water's surface.

Warning

Shock hazard can cause fatal injury. Always meet or exceed all electrical code requirements and exercise caution when working with electricity.

Plant foliage lit from beneath with low-voltage lights draws attention to the water feature after nightfall. As the surface floaters cover the surface with new foliage, the pond surface becomes a textured pattern of light, leaves, and water.

INSTALLING A 12-VOLT LIGHTING SYSTEM

Installing a 12-volt D.C. lighting system creates the most desirable effects, has the widest option choice, and is safer than A.C. electrical lighting systems. Always use an outdoor-rated transformer, plugged into a GFCI-protected, weatherproof outlet [see Installing an Electrical Supply to the Site, pg. 40]. Use direct-burial cable without protective conduit below ground and within the water feature. To install underwater fixtures, follow these steps:

1 Install a 12-volt D.C., weatherproof transformer at a GFCI-protected outlet attached to a weatherproof junction box. Plug in the transformer.

2 Excavate a trench 10 in. (25 cm) deep and 6 in. (15 cm) wide between the edge of the water feature and the transformer. Lay direct-burial 12–2 lighting cable in the trench.

3 Connect the direct-burial cable wire to the transformer using weatherproof, outdoor-rated connectors and fittings.

4 Adjust and position one or more lights in hidden locations within the feature, directing their light onto waterfalls or interesting surface plants.

5 Set the automatic timer on the transformer to turn the lights on at dusk and off when the hours of garden use end.

6 Low-voltage lighting kits, which include all the components needed for lighting a water feature, are available from both home centers and hardware stores.

Water gardens provide a wonderful opportunity to discover and nurture aquatic plants

Planting Aquatic Environments

It's best to plant most aquatic plants, including this 'Chameleon' variety of Houttuynia cordata, *in submersible containers or baskets with porous sides. This permits easy care, including quickly repositioning the plant in the feature and removing it for fertilizing, pest control, pruning, and deadheading.*

Now that you've installed your water feature, it's time to add its plants. Planting aquatic environments may be a new experience for you and, while most aspects are similar to planting other gardens, there are a few differences to add interest and discovery.

There are four types of aquatic plants, each suited for a different section of your water environment [see Aquatic Plants, pg. 16]. Some aquatic plants thrive near the water; others on, in, or below the surface of the water—most are rooted while some are free-floating. This chapter presents the requirements and demonstrates the garden installation techniques for each type of aquatic plant. You'll find ideas for selecting healthy aquatic plants at the nursery or garden center and gain insight into the suggested planting ratios to achieve the best water quality. Information is provided on the specialty containers and optimum soil required for installing submerged plants as well as for the proper preparation and placement of your in-ground plants growing at the shoreline.

Before choosing plants for your water garden, look to your garden plan and the volume of your water feature to understand the space you have available for aquatic plants. Decide the number needed of each type of plant based on the planting ratios presented in this chapter. These ratios comply with most design aesthetics and, more importantly, will help maintain your feature's water quality.

Like many gardening endeavors, growing aquatic plants has some unique challenges. For instance, some grow quickly—the more exuberant varieties easily can overtake younger, weaker species in a matter of weeks—and shoreline plants may require more frequent watering than do your other garden plants. Deep-water submersibles, marginals, and floaters, however, often require less care than your in-ground plants. On the whole, an aquatic environment provides an opportunity to cultivate your gardening skills, imagination, and passion.

AQUATIC ENVIRONMENTS

You'll choose and use plants in your water garden for both aesthetic and practical reasons. The first consideration is the aquatic environment you want to plant. Aquatic plants are defined by where they grow: on the shoreline, on top of the water, or submerged within the feature itself [see Aquatic Plants, pg. 16].

The next consideration is the same as for any garden: your site and climate conditions. You must choose plants that will thrive in your locale with the level of sun, shade, and wind found in your water garden. The United States Department of Agriculture [USDA] has divided the world into 11 zones based on their average minimum annual temperatures [see Plant Hardiness Around the World, pg. 115]. These zones roughly predict which plants will survive in a given area. You should choose plants that suit the plant hardiness zone of your water garden.

Plants require a certain pH from the soil or water where they live. The pH scale, measures acidity and alkalinity from 0–14, with 7.0 as neutral. Lower numbers indicate acid condtions, higher numbers alkaline. Relative acidity affects a plant's ability to absorb nutrients. Test soil and water prior to introducing plants [see Preparing Soil for Planting, pg. 61 and Testing and Treating Water, pg. 71].

Aquatic nursery and garden center staff will help you discover plants that will thrive in your garden and suit your other objectives, including your garden's intended purpose. Specific plant needs and their features are included in the plant listings found in the back of this book [see Encyclopedia of Aquatic Plants, pg. 79]. Consult them as you begin to choose plants for your water feature.

Select and cultivate aquatic plants in a careful ratio to achieve proper balance and a desirable appearance [see Planting Rations, this pg.]. Aquatic plants have a propensity to colonize quickly. Because plants growing in the water play a role in maintaining water quality, they must be thinned and pruned constantly to maintain proper oxygen levels, balanced water quality, and to avoid algae blooms. Always choose aquatic plants based on their mature height and spread in order to keep them in scale with the size of the feature. Even small water plants quickly grow in an hospitable water feature with ample sunlight, warmth, and nutrients.

PLANTING RATIOS

The correct ratio of aquatic plants to water feature area is key to achieving healthy water quality and an overall nurturing environment for plants, fish, and other living parts of your water garden. Maintain the following ratio of plants for each 50 square feet (4.6 m²) of water surface area. Such a blend will provide both aesthetic and practical benefits while keeping the aggressive varieties in check:

- Surface floaters = 6
- Submerged oxygenators = 15 bunches
- Shallow-depth marginals = 3
- Deep-depth marginals = 3
- Deep-water submersibles = 1

Aquatic plants are adapted by nature to live in different environments. In water gardens, risers are used to position plants at the proper depth. Aquatic plants include (left to right) deep-water submersibles, surface floaters, deep-depth marginals, above-water floaters, and shallow-depth marginals. Not shown: submerged oxygenator or shore-line plants.

SELECTING HEALTHY AQUATIC PLANTS

Use your garden plan, idea file, and the listings in this book to choose plants for your garden feature [see Encyclopedia of Aquatic Plants, pg. 79]. If you are new to the world of aquatic plants, seek out a specialty nursery as a source of both plants and information about them. To choose healthy plants suited to your garden and climate, follow these steps:

2 Choose plants bearing attractive foliage and textures, and with vibrant colored blooms. They also should have several new buds or emerging leaves.

1 Make a list of plants for each aquatic category best suited to your theme, your garden's plant hardiness zone, and your garden plan.

3 Avoid plants with discolored leaves or signs of pest infestation or disease. Choose only vigorous plants that appear strong.

4 Examine plants for clean, plump, and unstunted roots, often encased in a plastic bag with water to maintain an adequate moisture level.

5 Avoid plants that appear to be overly mature as these take longer to adjust to their new home in your water feature.

PREPARING TO PLANT

Generally, plant aquatic plants after the last frost, once warm spring temperatures have become established and are consistent. The exact date depends on your climate and, to a lesser degree, your desire to stagger blooms throughout the season.

In a natural environment, aquatic plants grow in the soil at the bottom of a pond or stream, or along its shoreline. There's a method for growing submerged and shoreline plants in soil within the liner. In fact, some rigid liners are molded with depressions in them to hold soil. The prevailing and preferred planting method, however, avoids placing soil directly into the liner. Keeping soil out of the liner eases thinning and fertilizing chores, lessens debris and loose soil that can clog pumps and filters, reduces overall soil needs, makes cleaning the liner easier for you and safer for your plants, and allows you to easily isolate sick plants.

Plant shoreline plants in amended native soil outside the edge of the liner, supplying frequent waterings to keep them moist. Some shoreline plants can be invasive, and some have soil needs different than typical garden soil. The solution for these issues is to install your plants in containers before burying them in the shoreline soil. Within the feature, pour floaters from their containers onto the water surface and let them float away or tether them with nylon fishing leader. Install marginals and deep-water submersibles in prepared soil placed into specialized shallow containers and topped by a thin coat of holding gravel. Submerge the container into the water of the feature to the depth required by the specific plant.

These specialized containers serve a purely functional purpose. Unseen and submerged underwater, plastic baskets or clay pots provide constant water intrusion while holding the plant's soil in place and keeping it at its proper depth. Marginal plants in containers often are set on shelves built into the liner. Deep-water submersibles generally are set at the bottom of the feature, but some plants require repositioning in the water as they grow. Set the container on risers—clay pots, plastic buckets, concrete blocks—and adjust as needed.

Wait 2–5 days after filling your feature with water before placing your plants into it. This allows water-treatment chemicals common in municipal supplies time to evaporate. The length of time needed depends on the feature's water volume. The water may turn green with algae, signaling that the water is ready to support plant life. As your plants grow, they will shade and stifle the algae, controlling it. Milky green water will transform into clear, with a healthy brown tint. If you are introducing fish into your water feature, first add chlorine-chloramine neutralizer, available at pet stores, to the water. Follow package instructions for dosage amounts and use.

Use caution when setting plants within the feature. Wear waders or soft-soled shoes—or go barefoot—and cushion the edges of the risers holding the planting containers, always seeking to prevent damage to the liner.

CHOOSING CONTAINERS

Many containers specifically manufactured for aquatic plants are available at nurseries and garden centers. They usually are baskets made of rigid or flexible plastic.

Other options include terra-cotta pots, natural fiber and woven willow baskets, and polypropylene bags punctured with copious drain holes.

Avoid metal containers that might corrode or leach into the water feature's environment. Also avoid solid containers that would restrict the flow of water and dissolved gasses to the plant's roots inside the containers.

Container baskets should allow water to easily flow through the soil and roots of aquatic plants. Most are made of durable polypropylene plastic.

PREPARING SOIL FOR PLANTING

Two distinctive soils are needed in and alongside water features. The soil for aquatic plants submerged within the liner generally should have moderate fertility, a dense texture, and permit water to easily penetrate to the plant roots. Shoreline plantings outside the liner require moist garden loam. To prepare your soil for planting, follow these steps:

Soil for Submerged Aquatic Plants

1 Mix equal parts of humus, sand, and sterile potting soil. Add a double portion of dry clay to the mix. This is your base soil.

2 Line a submersible container with porous landscape fabric and fill it with the soil mix. Soak it until saturated, washing away the smallest particles.

3 Soak the soil overnight in a basin of water. Floating organic material will become saturated and sink. Gently mix it into the soil.

Soil for Moist Shoreline Plants

1 Use a soil test kit, available at most garden stores, to test the nutrients and acid-alkaline balance of the soil, following its package instructions.

2 Amend the soil as directed by the test results and your plant needs. Shoreline plants generally require acidic 5.5–6.0 pH, achieved by adding peat or leafmold to overly alkaline soil. Improve texture by adding organic compost.

3 Complete your soil preparation by installing drip emitters around your feature. They will provide the regular irrigation needed to keep the soil moist.

PREPARING CONTAINERS AND BASKETS

Containers for aquatic plants serve a purely functional purpose. Unseen and submerged underwater, porous or woven plastic and fiber containers and baskets of various dimensions provide for constant water circulation, hold the soil in place, and maintain the plants at proper depth. To fill them with soil and protect them from erosion, follow these steps:

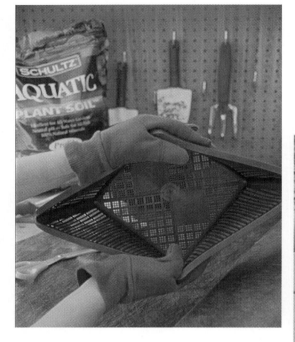

1 Inspect containers for any cracks, voids, or other structural damage. Clean containers thoroughly to remove any contaminants.

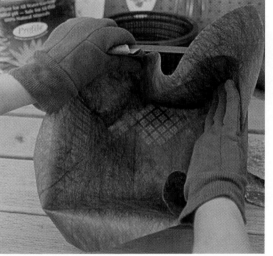

2 Install clean porous burlap or landscape fabric mesh along the inside of the container to contain the soil while allowing adequate moisture flow.

3 Weight the base of the container with dense stone. Heavy containers will prevent movement in currents.

4 Fill with the soil mix, leaving space for the plant roots and a layer 1–2 in. (25–50 mm) thick of pea gravel. Soak the container for 24 hours to exhaust air trapped in the soil and to saturate the organic elements.

PLANTING SUBMERGED AQUATIC PLANTS IN CONTAINERS

All submerged plants—marginal and deep-water—are planted in specialized containers in a similar manner before being installed into the water feature. First prepare the planting container [see pg. opposite]. Check your garden plan for the type, number of plants, and containers you'll need, and follow these steps:

1 Remove the thoroughly soaked container and its soil from the water basin. Gently mix the soil to incorporate any waterlogged organics that have settled on the soil surface.

2 Open a hole in the soil for the roots of the plant, removing some soil if necessary. Spread the roots and gently transplant it into the soil as you would other plants.

3 Gently pack the soil around the roots, adding soil as needed to cover them. Immerse the container in the water bath for a few minutes until bubbling stops, then remove and drain it. Fill all voids and replace any soil that has settled.

4 Add a layer of washed pea gravel topdressing 1–2 in. (25–50 mm) thick to the top of the container. It will protect the soil and further weight the container to prevent movement.

5 Set the plant in place in the feature, at a depth appropriate to the species. Stabilize and secure the container, using cobblestone from the feature.

6 Place immature aquatic plants on adjustable stands with their foliage just below the water. As the plants grow and leaves reach the surface, progressively lower the stand until it's at its final depth.

PLANTING MARGINAL AQUATICS IN THE LINER

Plant all submerged plants in their specialized containers [see Planting Submerged Aquatic Plants in Containers, pg. 63]. Then, install the plants into your water feature to their specified depth: shallow-depth marginals to 6 in. (15 cm) or less, deep-depth marginals 6–12 in. (15–30 cm) deep, and deep-water submersibles more than 1 ft. (30 cm) deep. To install submerged plants, follow these steps:

1 Install plants on the marginal shelves of the water feature, at the recommended depth for the species. Make sure the container is secure and stable on the shelf.

3 Plant invasive marginal plants in containers as you would other aquatic plants, then bury their containers inside separate liner pockets located at the edge of the feature. Provide a reliable source of water other than that from the feature, such as with drip irrigation.

2 For shallow-depth marginals, place the container so that the rim is slightly showing, which will allow water to lap over the edge while avoiding constant soil saturation.

4 If necessary, especially on hot days when the water may evaporate quickly, provide supplementary water to the perimeter plants with adequate drainage away from the water feature. If this is a recurring problem, add a layer of mulch around these plants to help retain moisture.

PLANTING SHORELINE PLANTS

Shoreline plants thrive in constantly moist conditions outside the liner. In nature they receive water from nearby ponds or streams. In a water garden, you must provide them with water. Test and prepare your soil [see Preparing Soil for Planting, pg. 61]. To plant them directly in the garden soil, follow these steps:

1 Install shoreline plants outside the lining of the water feature. Place them on the site in their nursery containers, spacing them according to your garden plan.

2 Dig holes 1 in. (25 mm) deeper and ⅓ wider than the nursery container. Add 5–10–10 starter fertilizer to the bottom of the hole as directed on the package, adding covering soil to prevent direct root contact.

3 Gently remove the plant from its nursery container. Invert the plant while supporting it with your palm. Tap the container and slide out the plant.

4 Set the plant into the hole with the top of its rootball even with the surrounding soil. Use a spade handle to gauge when the depth is right.

5 Firm the soil around the plant using your flattened palms. Water thoroughly, then repeat regularly until established. Maintain moist soil conditions with an irrigation system.

6 Plant invasive shoreline plants in containers as you would other aquatic plants, then bury their containers in the shoreline soil outside the liner. Provide a reliable source of water other than the feature, such as hand watering or a drip irrigation system.

A s with many garden projects, water garden care is timed to the seasons. Summer evaporation, for instance, may require you to replenish a pond's water to keep the pond full and its flexible liner from cracking, while winter presents issues of ice formation and plant protection. Spring, of course, brings the need for cleaning, adding new plants, and tending to fertilizing and promoting the new growth of your existing plants. Autumn signals the start of plant dormancy, pruning, and perhaps saying good-bye to migratory wildlife you've enjoyed.

Typically, aquatic plants are more carefree than their in-ground counterparts. In a water garden, however, plants are just part of what needs attention. The liner, systems, infrastructure, and finishing materials also require regular attention, maintenance, and repair.

This chapter provides information about regular water garden care. Step-by-step methods are shown for aquatic plant fertilizing and the testing and treating of water to help keep its quality high and your plants healthy. Every 1–3 years, your water feature will need a complete renovation: draining and cleaning, repairing the liner, and replanting, often with your thinned or divided plants. Easy methods showing how to do each of these water gardening tasks are presented as well.

If you live in a cold-winter area, you'll appreciate the tips on protecting your water feature and its plants during winter's freezing temperatures.

Although aquatic plants have strong defenses to pests and are nearly immune to many illnesses that infect in-ground plants, they sometimes fall prey to insects and disease. If you suspect pests or disease, look for guidance here as well.

Because you've properly located, designed, built, and planted your feature with species well-adapted to your USDA plant hardiness zone, you've bypassed many common water garden issues and limited your garden's need for care. Your reward is more time to enjoy the garden you've created.

> **Maintenance care of a water garden is keyed to logical changes that occur with seasonal cycles**

Water Garden Care

Use a subsurface water vacuum to remove settled plant debris and sediment from the water feature. Most ponds require minimal care: cleaning skimmer filters every two weeks, pruning dead leaves from plants, and inspecting them for pests or disease.

FERTILIZING SUBMERGED PLANTS

In a natural environment, the plants growing within the water receive nutrients from the natural decomposition of plant and animal life around them. In a typical water garden, marginal and deep-water submersible plants may require supplements of fertilizer or food until their ecosystem becomes balanced. Fertilizing aquatic plants requires precision both in choice of the fertilizer and its application. You'll want to avoid adding too many nutrient chemicals to the water itself, which may cause harm to plants that need few added nutrients, as well as to fish and other wildlife. Fertilizers may promote algae blooms and overstimulate plants that are best fed by natural processes.

There are four times to consider fertilizing: at planting, in the early part of the growing season to help aquatic plants emerge from dormancy, when plants are repotted after division or thinning, and when a specific plant shows signs of distress.

Each species of aquatic plant has specific nutrient needs [see Encyclopedia of Aquatic Plants, pg. 79]. Follow the advice of the aquatic specialist at your nursery or garden center for each species. Avoid using the same nutrients and application methods recommended for your in-ground plants; their needs are much different.

Use slow-release fertilizer tablets designed especially for aquatic plants. These tablets contain appropriate levels of nitrogen, potassium, phosphorous, and other nutrients. Check the package's instructions for the amount to apply. Embed the fertilizer tablets in the soil under the topdressing of gravel where they will dissolve slowly over time and remain, for the most part, within each plant's container. In addition, some nutrients can be spray-applied to the exposed leaves for immediate absorption, also in proper dilution and dosage.

You'll know if an individual plant is in need of fertilizer. It will become stunted, stop growing, or will display discolored or limp foliage. Remove the troubled plant and its container from the water and care for it individually. Inspect for signs of pests and disease before fertilizing and returning the plant to the water.

As you fertilize or otherwise treat your surrounding landscape—whether shoreline plants, nearby lawn, or vegetables—take care to avoid contaminating the feature's water with garden chemicals; they may alter or damage the delicate balance of the water and plants in your feature's ecosystem or cause algae to bloom.

Many aquatic plants spread new foliage from the moment that they are given a home in your water feature. They receive most of their nutrients from the water itself, recycling decayed plant matter. When their growth slows or leaves turn yellow, it may be time to fertilize.

FERTILIZING

Slow-release Fertilizer

1 Remove the plant from the water feature and allow it to drain. Use care to protect foliage from harm, especially when handling large plants.

W hile most submerged aquatic plants get the bulk of their nutrients from the water, marginals occasionally require extra boosts from fertilizer because most of their growth occurs above the water surface. Condition the soil of young, overwintered, divided, or repotted plants with encapsulated slow-release granules. Fertilize the plants every two months during the growing season. Wear a pair of long rubber gloves, poke fertilizer pellets into the damp soil, and follow these instructions:

2 Apply slow-release tablets for aquatic plants and the species. Insert tablet into the soil below the gravel topdressing, as directed on the fertilizer package.

3 Replace the fertilized plant in the water feature. Fan its foliage, eliminating tangles or inverted leaves.

Liquid Foliar Fertilizer

1 Spray-apply liquid foliar fertilizer on floating and standing foliage monthly during the growing season. Allow the foliage to dry completely before returning plants to the water feature.

WATER QUALITY AND ALGAE

Balanced water quality is essential to maintaining a healthy water garden. Balance is achieved by establishing proper plant ratios, maintaining the water level, controlling debris and other organic matter, and testing regularly for the optimal pH and telltale nutrient levels of the water.

Choose plants selectively, and control their growth on a regular basis [see Planting Ratios, pg. 58]. Always keep your water feature filled to its correct depth. When your water turns from clear to green, that's algae thriving in nutrient-rich water and sunlight. It signals a healthy, fertile aquatic environment ready to support more desirable plant life; balance your feature with a proper mix of plants. Once they are in and begin to grow, the algae will subside, and the water will turn to a rich amber.

Look for these common symptoms of water quality distress:

- Red water—algae
- Brown water—loose or stirred-up sediment
- Black water—decayed leaves
- Milky water—organic decay
- Rainbow slick—presence of oil
- Drooping plants—herbicide draining into water
- Failure to thrive—improper pH or soil mix
- Excess growth—excess nitrite in the water
- Stunted growth—excess nitrite or ammonia in water

Use a reagent test kit to test your water regularly for its pH—the water's acid-alkaline balance—and nitrate, nitrite, and ammonia levels. Nitrite from plant decomposition converts by chlorophyll photosynthesis to nitrate, a stable form. Excess nitrite signals too much fertilizer in the water, a condition that causes algae to grow and quickly will turn the water green. It's also important to check ammonia levels in the water. Ammonia from fish and animal waste can stunt plants and kill fish. Test for ammonia and, if it is detected, take steps immediately to remove it from the water (see Testing and Treating Water, opposite pg].

Water quality may be difficult to judge when algae blooms cloud the water feature with unwanted growth. A good crop of algae reveals that the water likely has excess nutrients, sunlight, and oxygen that would better be channeled into growing your aquatic plants.

Reagent test kits are used to test water quality for several telltale compounds that reveal the water's quality. Test kits are available at nurseries, garden centers, and aquarium stores.

TESTING AND TREATING WATER

If plants appear droopy or discolored, and the feature's water is an unhealthy shade, it's time to remedy the situation. Ponds are more likely to become too alkaline and build up excess nitrite than to contain ammonia. Take these steps before resorting to chemicals or performing a complete clean-out:

1 Study the feature. Its water color and surface should be clear, tinted amber. Plants should be vital and green and healthy. Algae blooms and weakened plants denote excess nitrate in the water or high pH.

2 Take samples to test the acid-alkaline balance of the water. Test kits and electronic pH meters are available at garden centers. Optimum pH levels are 6.5–7.5 on a scale of 14.

3 Test the water's nitrate and nitrite level using reagent test strips or liquid test kits, available at water garden suppliers. The relative balance reveals the feature's nutrients.

4 Also test the water's ammonia content, which should be zero. If ammonia is present due to plant or animal waste, exchange 10–20% of the feature's water every 3–5 days until the test is negative.

5 Remove and wash the feature's biologic filter media. Clean the skimmer of accumulated debris. Exchange 20% of the water; use of a chlorine or chloramine neutrilizer generally is unnecessary for small water exchanges. Retest after 24 hours.

PERIODIC MAINTENANCE

In a natural environment, ponds and streams develop a sustainable ecosystem. In a water garden, the components—liners, pumps, filters, fountains—require regular maintenance to make sure they're performing at peak levels. A water garden's maintenance schedule follows the seasons.

Spring is preparation time: Clean and repair liners, pumps, and other devices. Inspect plants as they emerge from dormancy. Prune shoreline plants to encourage new growth. Thin, divide, and replant submerged plants.

Summer is the growing season: Enjoy aquatic plants as they thrive in the heat and light of the sun. Keep shoreline plants well watered. Maintain the water level within the feature, making sure the top of the liner remains protected by the water and edging materials. Inspect plants for any signs of pest and disease. Check water quality regularly.

Autumn signals the onset of the plants' dormancy period: Unless you live in an extremely cold climate, leave your plants in place. Keep the water at its proper level and its quality in balance. Consider thinning, pruning, or dividing plants. In regions with cold-winter climates, perform necessary maintenance to protect your water feature, prevent ice from forming and damaging the liner, and keep a hole open so that air can be exchanged [see Winterizing in Cold Climates, pg. 75].

PUMP MAINTENANCE

Your pump, its filter, delivery pipe, and housing should be checked semimonthly and may need to be cleaned out once a month: check the pump manufacturer's package literature for a recommended schedule. Use a garden hose spray nozzle to clean the housing and filter media, replacing the filter and screen, if necessary. Also check for any leaks or damage. If you plan to store the pump over the winter, keep it in a bucket of cool water so that its internal works and gaskets remain soft and supple.

(Top) Winter is a dormant time for most aquatic plants in those areas that experience freezing temperatures. Hardy perennial aquatic plants winter best inside the pond if an air hole remains open to freshen the water.

(Bottom) Spring marks the beginning of the growing season. Clean away debris left from winter and check that plants are securely positioned in the water feature as they begin to send up new shoots.

CLEANING A POND

1 Detach the pump discharge connection, leaving it in place, and replace it with a temporary drain hose. Use the pump to drain the feature. If it is in a skimmer box, relocate it to the main pond.

Water features will operate reliably for long periods. Clean them completely only every 2–3 years. It's time to clean when the water quickly becomes unbalanced and fails quality tests, the bottom is sediment-filled, and the liner is algae-coated [see Testing and Treating Water, pg. 71]. Clean the feature on an overcast day in late spring or early summer, to allow time for plants to recover before going dormant. To clean a water feature, follow these steps:

2 Gently remove plants and fish, placing them in nearby water tubs or buckets as the pond empties. They will be out of the pond for several days. Use this opportunity to inspect them for pest and disease damage or need for thinning and pruning.

3 If you keep fish, net and place them in temporary tanks as they collect in the deepest areas of the feature. Once all fish and plants are taken out, gently remove remaining water by hand.

4 Use your hands, clean rags, and soft sponges to remove all silt, debris, and other decayed matter from the bottom of the pond. Wash off the protective gravel and boulders. Avoid using tools that might puncture the liner.

5 Check for leaks, damage, or signs of wear. Replace the protective gravel and boulders. Reposition plants.

6 Refill the pond with water. Allow a few days for the chemical additives in your municipal water to dissipate and evaporate before replacing your plants and fish.

REPAIRING LINER LEAKS

1 Drain, remove plants and fish, and clean the feature to expose any leaks or signs of damage or wear. Remove the protective gravel, cobble, and boulders from the area suspected of leaks, exposing the liner.

Liner leaks result from inadvertent punctures, sharp objects falling in the water, roots growing through the underlayment into the liner, animal tunneling, and basic wear and tear. Regular maintenance checks of your water garden should include leak inspection. Look for wear points, unexpected low water, saturated soil outside the liner, and soil in the bottom of the feature. To repair a liner leak, follow these steps:

2 Thoroughly clean the area around the puncture with clean water, rinse, and dry. Further clean the patch area with denatured alcohol or an adhesive primer.

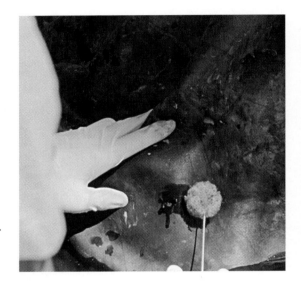

3 Choose a suitable repair kit matched to the liner material. Patch the affected area following the package instructions. Extend all patches 2–4 in. (50–100 mm) beyond the immediate puncture area.

4 Apply a coat of an aquarium-grade silicone sealant over the repaired area to protect the patch and isolate it from the feature's water. Allow patch and sealant to dry thoroughly.

WINTERIZING IN COLD CLIMATES

1 As ice begins to form on the surface, install a small heater or auxilliary submersible pump near the surface of the water to prevent ice formation and allow ample oxygen to enter the water.

As winter arrives in cold-winter climates, your water feature requires protection from cold temperatures and ice. Hardy, dormant aquatic plants should remain in the feature; tropicals should be removed to a warm, indoor location. Protect the liner from ice and freezing damage to the pump, pipes, or filters. A natural exchange of air is essential to maintain water quality. Before the first frost, follow these steps:

2 Leave submersible pumps operating in the feature. Protect above-ground recirculating lines from freezing. Wrap them with heat-tape or insulation. Moving water resists ice formation. Turn off and drain above-ground pumps and lines, installing a small submersible pump in the feature.

3 Most outdoor fish species will congregate around the heater and open water areas. Dissolved oxygen supplies are most plentiful in the open water area, and the circulating water carries oxygen to all the feature's areas and its plants.

4 If cold temperatures become extreme, it sometimes is necessary to add plastic foam float blocks to flex against ice expansion that otherwise would damage the liner. Leave at least 20% of the surface open.

PESTS AND DISEASES

Diseases and insects happen even in the best water features. The combination of the water's natural nutrients and the variety of plant foliage makes a fitting habitat for fungal diseases and a fine feast for pests. Knowing the steps to take to prevent and control infestations and infections before they become severe will ensure the health of your feature and avoid use of garden chemicals.

Pest control begins with a healthy garden, both in the plant life and the water. Choose appropriate plants and provide them consistent care. Although all aquatic plants have some natural resistance to infections, those varieties that are adapted to your USDA plant hardiness zone are most adept at naturally resisting your area's pests and illnesses. Prevent garden infestations by using sterile soil mixes every time you add a new plant to the garden; reused containers and garden soil often contain fungal spores that spread disease.

A healthy garden environment is better able to resist pests and diseases. Maintaining overall plant health, ensuring water quality, and regularly removing debris in and around the water goes a long way toward prevention of the most common conditions.

In addition, make periodic inspections of your plants and water, turning over leaves to discover signs of illness and digging into the soil in submerged containers to expose insect pests. Infested or ill plants should be removed from the garden promptly, then cared for away from other plants. Always clean your equipment and gloves after working on ill plants to maintain the health of other parts of your garden, both aquatic and on land.

If the pest infestation or disease infection is severe or spreading, consider pesticides and fungicides applied to the ill aquatic plants. Avoid applying such measures to the pond as a whole; treat only the plants bearing signs of damage or disease, isolated in a location outside the pond.

Aquatic plants have insect pests that can strip leaves and stems, cut holes in foliage, or otherwise attack the plants. Frequent inspection and early discovery are the best ally to prevent a major infestation from becoming established or spreading.

If you keep fish or your feature supports other wildlife, keep the treated plants out of the pond until the control agent's package instructions specifically state that any hazard has abated.

All pesticides are designed to be effective on particular pests, and fungicides address specific diseases. Check labels before use for a listing of your plant's specific condition. Always wear protective clothing when applying garden chemicals. Target the affected areas in package-recommended doses and dilutions. Dispose of chemicals and applicators as recommended by the manufacturer when you're done.

When the infestation has been reduced, the plants returned to health, and no more applications are required, reintroduce the plants to your water feature. Wait an additional 24–48 hours before reintroducing any fish, amphibians, or aquatic reptiles to the feature.

HEALING SICK PLANTS

Awatchful eye is first aid for healing plants. The sooner a pest infestation or disease infection is discovered, the sooner you can take action to control it. Accurate identification is key to effective pesticide and fungicide use. Rely on the staff at your nursery or garden center to help you treat your plants. To heal marginal and deep-water submersible plants, follow these steps:

1 Collect a piece of damaged foliage in a plastic bag and seek identification help from your nursery or garden center.

2 Create a temporary holding basin to isolate affected plants. Remove sick plants from the water feature and place them in the holding basin.

3 Hand pick insect pests from foliage. This may be sufficient to control many pests.

4 If hand control methods fail, choose a pesticide or fungicide that specifically lists the pest or disease. Wear protective clothing and gloves, and apply the control following completely and exactly all of the package label instructions.

5 Once the plant is healthy and all residue of the control agent has abated as indicated on the product's label instructions, replace the plant in your water feature.

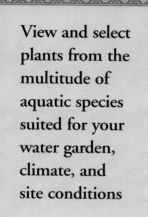

View and select plants from the multitude of aquatic species suited for your water garden, climate, and site conditions

An n exciting array of aquatic plants awaits planting in water gardens. The following pages feature many plants for ponds, pools, streams, and watercourses. Using this encyclopedia, you will find a perfect plant for every environment in, on, and around your water feature. Plants exist to suit every style of garden design and thrive in every growing region.

You can use this encyclopedia in several ways. View the photographs and read their detailed descriptions to discover plants that have the size, texture, and bloom color that suit your needs. Note plants that grow well in your USDA plant hardiness zone [see Plant Hardiness Around the World, pg. 115]. Find individual plants that best suit your garden purpose such as night bloomers, those attractive to birds, or easy-care plants. All the information you need can be found in a quick glance at these pages.

Each plant is listed by its common names first, permitting you to quickly identify your favorites. Because some plants are known by different regional names, several common names are listed for some plants. For garden center staff and professional horticulturists, the scientific name is noted as well. All names are found in the back of the book [see Index, pg. 118].

Encyclopedia of Aquatic Plants

Along with a beautiful photograph, every listing carries the most essential information about each plant. Before choosing one for your garden, read about its ideal habitat, eventual size, general look, and the USDA plant hardiness zones where it grows best. Before planting, verify the plant's soil needs, sun and other exposure requirements, and spacing from other plants. After the plant is in place, use the listings to check on care recommendations. Look to the features category for ideal placement and garden location ideas. Also noted are garden styles that best suit the plants, along with other interesting and helpful information about the individual plants.

Choose from Variegated Water Clover, Water Lily, Summer Crocus, or Ribbon Grass, just a few among the 93 aquatic plants found on the pages that follow.

Common name: Alder, Black
Scientific name: *Alnus glutinosa*
Habitat/Size: Shoreline, moist to saturated soil. Grows to 80 ft. (25 m) tall.
Description: Deciduous tree. Creates a thicket of branches from the ground up, forming a narrow pyramid with a raggedy top when mature. Deep furrows and checkers etch the dark brown bark. Tassels of male catkins, followed by female cones, decorate the bare winter branches. Spring blooming.
Plant hardiness: Zones 3–9.
Soil needs: Moist. Fertility: Poor, tolerates lime. 6.0–8.0 pH.
Planting: Full sun to partial shade. 10 ft. (3 m) apart. Submerge at least 1 ft. (30 cm) deep.
Care: Thrives in poor, wet locations.
Features: Good choice for accents, arrangements, screens. Long-lasting leaves. Cultivars offer different forms. Attracts birds.

Common name: Anemone
Scientific name: *Anemone rivularis*
Habitat/Size: Shoreline. Grows to 3 ft. (90 cm) tall, 1 ft. (30 cm) wide.
Description: Woody perennial. Tall flower stalks, with leaf pairs at intervals, bear 2–5 delicate blossoms, ½–1½ in. (13–38 mm) wide, white with a blue outer wash. Late spring to early summer blooming.
Plant hardiness: Zones 6–9.
Soil needs: Moist, sandy, well-drained. Fertility: Average. 6.0–8.0 pH.
Planting: Full sun to partial shade. 1 ft. (30 cm) apart. Refrigerate seeds 3–5 weeks, plant in late winter, 1–6 months to germinate.
Care: Water regularly. Divide in late summer.
Features: Good choice for accents, cut flowers, frames for garden accessories, screens in natural gardens. Use in masses to blend plantings from water feature to other garden areas. Flowers move beautifully in a slight breeze, adding motion to the garden. Dormant in winter.

Common name: Arrowhead; Duck Potato
Scientific name: *Sagittaria latifolia*
Habitat/Size: Shallow-depth marginal. Grows 2–4 ft. (60–120 cm) tall.
Description: Tuberous perennial. Handsome narrow leaves 4–12 in. (10–30 cm) long grow on long stalks, angle upward above the surface. Whorls of 3 bright white, yellow-centered flowers open on a leafless stem. July and August blooming.
Plant hardiness: Zones 3–11.
Soil needs: Loam. Fertility: Average. 6.0–8.0 pH.
Planting: Full sun to shade in hot regions. 1 ft. (30 cm) apart. Submerge 6 in. (15 cm) deep.
Care: Plant bulbs in spring. Divide tuberous roots in summer.
Features: Good choice for natural gardens. Provides interesting texture at water's surface. North American native. Native peoples once ate the tubers. Water lily aphid susceptible.

Common name: Arum, Arrow

Scientific name: *Peltandra virginica*

Habitat/Size: Shoreline, shallow-depth marginal. Grows to 3 ft. (90 cm) tall, 2 ft. (60 cm) wide.

Description: Hardy perennial. Big glossy leaves 6–36 in. (15–90 cm) long, 4–8 in. (10–20 cm) wide. Narrow flowers 8 in. (20 cm) long, cream-edged green with yellow centers. Red berries in autumn.

Plant hardiness: Zones 5–9.

Soil needs: Loam, high in organic matter, lime-free. Fertility: Rich. 6.0 pH.

Planting: Full sun to partial shade. 3 ft. (90 cm) apart. Submerge 6 in. (15 cm) deep.

Care: Plant rhizomes on shoreline in spring or summer, sow seed in submerged containers. Divide in spring.

Features: Good choice for accents by ponds. Native to swamps and streams of southeast U.S.

> **Warning**
>
> All parts of arum cause skin and mouth irritation, digestive upset if ingested.

Common name: Baby's Tears

Scientific name: *Micranthemum* species

Habitat/Size: Shoreline, shallow-depth marginal, deep-depth marginal. Grows to 1 ft. (30 cm) tall.

Description: Three species of creeping, herbaceous annuals. Clumps of slender stems, crowded with round, succulent ¼-in. (6-mm) leaves.

Plant hardiness: Zone varies by species.

Soil needs: Moist to wet. Fertility: Average. 5.5–8.0 pH.

Planting: Partial sun to full shade, best with filtered light. Clusters 6 in. (15 cm) apart. Submerge 3–8 in. (75–200 mm) deep.

Care: Control by thinning or division.

Features: Good choice for borders of slow-moving stream. *M. umbrosum* is the most popular water garden plant. North American native.

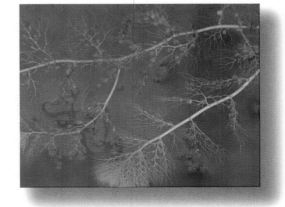

Common name: Bladderwort

Scientific name: *Utricularia* species

Habitat/Size: Shoreline, shallow-depth marginal, deep-depth marginal. Grows in dense, short mats.

Description: About 200 species of aquatic or terrestrial herbs. Plants produce hundreds of inflated traps on branching stems of small leaves. Tiny flowers above floating bladders. Summer blooming.

Plant hardiness: Zone varies by species.

Soil needs: Moist, peat-sand mixture. Fertility: Average. 6.0–8.0 pH.

Planting: Full sun to partial shade. Still or slow-moving water. Spacing varies by species.

Care: Divide in spring or summer. May self-seed. Can be invasive.

Features: Good choice for ground cover. When a tiny water creature triggers sensory hairs, the floating trap snaps shut. Folklore of mosquito control is a myth.

Common name: Bogbean; Marsh Trefoil
Scientific name: *Menyanthes trifoliata*
Habitat/Size: Shoreline, shallow-depth marginal. Grows to 8 in. (20 cm) tall.
Description: Perennial. A low-growing creeper, it raises red stems above the water, bearing erect, fresh green leaves in threes. Small clusters of pink buds open into tiny, fringed white flowers. May blooming.
Plant hardiness: Zones 3–10.
Soil needs: Wet, peaty. Fertility: Average. 5.0–6.0 pH.
Planting: Full sun to partial shade. 16 in. (40 cm) apart. Submerge to 6 in. (15 cm) deep.
Care: Fully frost-hardy. Keep seeds moist and sow late winter to early spring, with the pot just submerged in water. Divide in spring or root cuttings in summer. Fast-spreading, branching rhizomes can be very invasive.
Features: Good choice for edges. Adds appealing three-dimensional pattern reflecting on water surface.

Common name: Bugleweed, Carpet; Ajuga
Scientific name: *Ajuga reptans*
Habitat/Size: Shoreline. Grows 4–6 in. (10–15 cm) tall.
Description: Creeping perennial, evergreen in mild climates. Dense mat of small, oval, deep green leaves turn, reddish bronze in autumn. Slender stalks with clusters of tiny blue, pink, or white flowers. Spring and summer blooming.
Plant hardiness: Zones 4–9.
Soil needs: Sandy, loam, clay, moist, well-drained. Fertility: Rich. 6.0–7.0 pH
Planting: Full sun to full shade. 6–12 in. (15–30 cm) apart. Can be invasive on shoreline; plant in containers and bury in soil.
Care: Water moderately. Divide after first spring growth.
Features: Good choice for borders, ground cover. Makes an excellent transition from sun around water feature to shady areas of the garden. Crown rot susceptible.

Common name: Bulrush; Woolgrass
Scientific name: *Scirpus cyperinus*
Habitat/Size: Shoreline, shallow-depth marginal. Grows 3–5 ft. (90–150 cm) tall.
Description: Shaggy, russet brown seed tassels arch gracefully on sturdy stems above a dense fountain of narrow leaf blades reaching 3 ft. (90 cm) long. Seed tassels turn woolly when in fruit. Summer blooming.
Plant hardiness: Zones 3–11.
Soil needs: Moist to wet. Fertility: Poor. 6.0–8.0 pH.
Planting: Full sun to partial shade. 2 ft. (60 cm) apart. Can be invasive on shoreline; plant in containers and bury in soil.
Care: Control self-sowing by cutting flower stems.
Features: Good choice for natural gardens. Adds height, interesting texture, and movement to the garden.

Common name: Buttercup
Scientific name: *Ranunculus* species
Habitat/Size: Shoreline. Grows to 2 ft. (60 cm).
Description: About 250 species of annuals, biennials, and perennials, some of which thrive in aquatic environments. Alternate, lobed, or divided leaves. Single, some double flowers, usually yellow. Plants with white flowers tend to be aquatic. Summer blooming. Head of small fruit is ornamental.
Plant hardiness: Zones 3–6.
Soil needs: Moist, well-drained. Fertility: Average. 7.0 pH.
Planting: Partial to full shade. Spacing depends on species.
Care: Water moderately. Propagate from seeds, division in spring.
Features: Good choice for ground cover in shade areas around water feature, especially in woodland gardens.

Common name: Canna
Scientific name: *Canna* species
Habitat/Size: Shoreline, shallow-depth marginal. Grows 4–6 ft. (1.2–1.8 m) tall.
Description: About 60 species of tender tropical perennials. Big spade-shaped leaves, many in bronze or purple hues. Produces vivid, orchidlike blossoms. Cultivars offer variegated leaves and flowers in brilliant yellows, reds, oranges with splashes of contrasting colors. Summer blooming.
Plant hardiness: Zones 9–11; 7–8 with protection.
Soil needs: Moist to wet, high in organic matter. Fertility: Rich. 6.0–8.0 pH.
Planting: Full sun, sheltered from wind, steady warmth and humidity. 18 in. (45 cm) apart. Submerge 3–4 in. (75–100 mm) deep.
Care: Keep roots wet. Enrich soil with manure and feed phosphate-rich fertilizer twice monthly in growing season. Water generously while blooming. In frost zones, lift brittle rhizomes and dry, store in sawdust or vermiculite kept slightly moist. Start rhizomes in indoor containers in early spring, plant after frost danger is past.
Features: Good choice for accents, massing in tropical gardens.

Common name: Cardinal Flower; Indian Pink
Scientific name: *Lobelia Cardinalis*
Habitat/Size: Shoreline. Grows 1–3 ft. (30–90 cm) tall.
Description: Perennial. Long, deep green leaves may have a bronzy tinge. Bright scarlet flowers, with long petal lobes flaring from a narrow tube, top a tall stalk. August to October blooming.
Plant hardiness: Zones 3–10.
Soil needs: Moist, loam. Fertility: Rich. 6.0–8.0 pH.
Planting: Full sun to partial shade. Sheltered from wind. 1 ft. (30 cm) apart. Avoid very wet winter conditions.
Care: Keep moist. In boggy soil or cold-winter climates, lift before onset of winter and store until spring. Add manure to soil before planting. Sow fresh seeds in autumn, divide clumps in spring; plants sprout from buried nodes.
Features: Good choice for edges. Short lived. North American native.

Common name: Cattail
Scientific name: *Typha* species
Habitat/Size: Deep-depth marginal. Grows 4–8 ft. (1.2–2.4 m) tall.
Description: About 15 species of perennials. The quintessential tall marsh plant, its familiar stems of sausage-shaped catkins sway and tap against each other above rustling, straplike leaves.
Plant hardiness: Zones 3–6.
Soil needs: Wet, rich in organic matter. Fertility: Rich. 6.0–8.0 pH.
Planting: Full sun to partial shade. 2 ft. (60 cm) apart. Submerge 1 ft. (30 cm) deep.
Care: Very frost-hardy. Grow from seed or divide in spring.
Features: Good choice for backdrop to shorter plants, cut flowers. Stabilizes a bank, but may be invasive if planted on shoreline.

Common name: Cattail, Miniature
Scientific name: *Typha minima*
Habitat/Size: Shallow-depth marginal, deep-depth marginal. Grows to 15 in. (38 cm) tall.
Description: Perennial. This dwarf version of the quintessential marsh plant is ideal for smaller residential gardens. Bears diminutive sausage-shaped catkins, rustling, straplike leaves 1 in. (25 mm) long.
Plant hardiness: Zones 3–6.
Soil needs: Wet, rich in organic matter. Fertility: Rich. 6.0–8.0 pH.
Planting: Full sun to partial shade. 1 ft. (30 cm) apart. Submerge 6–8 in. (15–20 cm) deep.
Care: Very frost-hardy. Grow from seed or divide in spring.
Features: Good choice for cut flowers, small-scale sites. Less invasive than the full-size species.

Common name: Chameleon
Scientific name: *Houttuynia cordata* 'Chameleon'
Habitat/Size: Shallow-depth marginal. Grows 1–2 ft. (30–60 cm) tall.
Description: Perennial. A colorful spreading ground cover with neat appearance. Aromatic heart-shaped leaves on red stems are variegated green and yellow when young, later develop red margins and splotches. White bracts enclose tiny yellow flowers. Summer blooming. Dies away in winter.
Plant hardiness: Zones 4–11; 3–5 as an annual.
Soil needs: Moist, cool, porous. Fertility: Average. 6.0–8.0 pH.
Planting: Full sun to shade in hot climates. 1 ft. (30 cm) apart. Submerge 2–4 in. (50–100 mm) deep.
Care: Plant ripe seed, cuttings, new fibrous shoots in late spring to early summer. Can overwinter as a houseplant.
Features: Good choice for adding vivid color to a shady shoreline. Develops best variegation with good light. Crushed leaves smell of orange peel.

Common name: Creeping Jenny; Moneywort
Scientific name: *Lysimachia Nummularia*
Habitat/Size: Shoreline, shallow-depth marginal. Grows 3–10 in. (75–250 mm) tall, stems to 20 in. (50 cm) long.
Description: Creeping perennial. Pairs of coinlike leaves form a dense, vivid green mat. Cup-shaped, single golden flowers bloom on short stalks. Midsummer blooming.
Plant hardiness: Zones 3–8.
Soil needs: Moist, rich in organic matter. Fertility: Rich. 6.0–8.0 pH.
Planting: Full sun to partial shade. 9–18 in. (23–45 cm) apart. Submerge 1 in. (25 mm) over crown.
Care: Sow seed in late summer, divide established plants autumn to spring. Enrich soil with manure at planting.
Features: Good choice for accents, dangling over rocks or walls, ground cover that takes light foot traffic. Popular 'Aurea' features pale golden leaves, deepening to lime green in shade.

Common name: Crocus, Summer
Scientific name: *Zephyranthes* species
Habitat/Size: Shoreline. Grows 3–6 in. (75–150 mm) tall.
Description: About 75 species of small, Iris family corms. Grasslike, medium green leaves. Yellow, lavender, white, purple flowers are cup-shaped on long tubes, appearing stemless, 1½–3 in. (38–75 mm) long. Most are late winter to early spring blooming; a few varieties also bloom in autumn. Some are pungently fragrant.
Plant hardiness: Zones 3–9; best in cold-winter areas.
Soil needs: Well-drained. Fertility: Average. 7.0 pH.
Planting: Partial shade. 2–3 in. (50–75 mm) apart, 3–5 in. (75–130 mm) deep.
Care: Protect from rodents. Plant in autumn. Propagate from division.
Features: Good choice for edges of water feature, massing between water feature and other areas of the garden.

Common name: Duckweed, Star; Ivy-Leaf Duckweed
Scientific name: *Lemna trisulca*
Habitat/Size: Submerged oxygenator. Dense mats.
Description: Perennial. Chains of tiny green leaves carpet the pond in spongy mats resting just under the surface. Fronds break off to form new colonies. Lacks roots. Rarely forms flowers.
Plant hardiness: Zones 4–11.
Soil needs: Water rich in lime and nitrates. 6.0–8.0 pH.
Planting: Full sun to partial shade. Best in still water.
Care: Set starting colonies onto the pond. Skim off excess growth to control. Clean fronds from bottom of feature to prevent pump and filter clogs. Tolerates a wide range of water temperatures.
Features: Good choice for fish ponds, wildlife gardens. Provides cover for young fish; food for fish, ducks, and other birds. Can be somewhat invasive.

Common name: Elephant's Ear; Green Taro
Scientific name: *Colocasia esculenta*
Habitat/Size: Shoreline. Grows to 6 ft. (1.8 m) tall.

Description: Deciduous perennial. Huge leaves grow to 2 ft. (60 cm) long, 15 in. (38 cm) wide from edible starchy tubers. Flower 6–14 in. (15–35 cm) wide hides among the leaves, followed by green berries.
Plant hardiness: Zones 10–11; 3–9 as an annual.
Soil needs: Moist, clay. Fertility: Rich. 5.5–6.5 pH.
Planting: Full sun to partial shade. Sheltered from wind. 4 ft. (1.2 m) apart.
Care: Water generously and provide diluted fertilizer monthly during summer growth. Where temperatures drop below 70°F (21°C), remove tubers to overwinter; replant in spring.
Features: Good choice for accents, borders. Source of Hawaiian poi, taro chips.

> **Warning**
>
> Sap of taro contains a skin irritant. Wear gloves to harvest. Boiling, baking, or roasting neutralizes the irritant.

Common name: Fern, Royal
Scientific name: *Osmunda regalis*
Habitat/Size: Shoreline. Grows 3–6 ft. (90–180 cm) tall, 3 ft. (90 cm) wide.
Description: Bold fern bears a crown of coarse green fronds on tall stems. Russet brown spore-bearing flower stalks rise above the sterile fronds.
Plant hardiness: Zones 3–9.
Soil needs: Moist to wet, clay or medium loam. Fertility: Average. 6.0 pH.
Planting: Partial to full shade. 3 ft. (90 cm) apart.
Care: Fast-growing. Dies back in cold winters. Let spent fronds remain as winter mulch.
Features: Good choice for accents, borders, background in native, tropical gardens. Just one plant provides excellent background screen for ponds, streams. Naturalizes to form a dense stand. Fibrous roots used as orchid-potting medium. Deer-resistant. North American native.

Common name: Forget-Me-Not, Water
Scientific name: *Myosotis scorpioides*
Habitat/Size: Shoreline. Grows 1–3 ft. (30–90 cm) tall.
Description: Perennial. The true forget-me-not, its shiny, bright green leaves make a good ground cover. Clusters of vivid blue flowers, with central eyes of white, yellow, pink. May to July blooming.
Plant hardiness: Zones 5–10.
Soil needs: Moist to wet, clay. Fertility: Average. 6.0–8.0 pH.
Planting: Full sun, wet soil to full shade, moist soil. 1–2 ft. (30–60 cm) apart.
Care: Frost-hardy. Sow in late spring, divide, root cuttings. Fertilize before flowering. Self-sows.
Features: Good choice for ground cover, it spreads readily over wet ground. Thrives in heavy clay at the pond edge. Deer-resistant. Dwarf cultivar 'Semperflorens' grows to 8 in. (20 cm) tall.

Common name: Frogfruit, Northern; Fog-fruit
Scientific name: *Phyla lanceolata*
Habitat/Size: Shoreline, shallow-depth marginal. Grows to 2 ft. (60 cm) long, 6 in. (15 cm) tall.
Description: Creeping herbaceous perennial. Oblong, bright green leaves grow 3 in. (75 mm) long. Leafless spikes grow 2 in. (50 mm) tall topped with small, purple-centered, white or blue flowers. May to September blooming.
Plant hardiness: Zones 4–9.
Soil needs: Moist. Fertility: Average. 6.0–7.0 pH.
Planting: Partial shade. Submerge to 6 in. (15 cm).
Care: Easy. Prune to control growth.
Features: Good choice for ground cover in wet areas, prairies, shade gardens. Provides shelter for amphibians. Southern U.S. and Mexico native.

Common name: Frog's-bit, American
Scientific name: *Limnobium Spongia*
Habitat/Size: Surface floater, shallow-depth marginal. Grows leaves to 2½ in. (63 mm), stems to 8 in. (20 cm).
Description: Round, leathery leaves form buoyant, dense mat. Younger leaves are heart-shaped, shiny green above and reddish beneath. Tiny, spidery white flowers bloom below the leaves.
Plant hardiness: Zones 5–11.
Soil needs: Loam. Fertility: Average. 6.0–8.0 pH.
Planting: Full sun. 1 ft. (30 cm) apart. Submerge 6 in. (15 cm) deep.
Care: Divide clumps regularly. Can be invasive in warmer climates.
Features: Good choice for edges. Grown for foliage. Grows as a floater in natural environments, but does best when rooted. North American native. Similar looking to *Hydrocharis morsus-ranae*, Frogbit, an invasive nuisance plant banned in many areas.

Common name: Globeflower
Scientific name: *Trollius europaeus*
Habitat/Size: Shoreline. Grows 18–24 in. (45–60 cm) tall, 18 in. (45 cm) wide.
Description: Compact perennial. Erect, hollow stems bear finely cut, toothed, shiny, dark green leaves. Single, cuplike, light lemon to rich yellow flowers 2 in. (50 mm) wide. Late spring to early summer blooming.
Plant hardiness: Zones 5–9.
Soil needs: Deep, loam or clay loam, rich in organic matter. Fertility: Rich. 5.8–6.8 pH.
Planting: Full sun to partial shade. 18 in. (45 cm) apart.
Care: Very frost-hardy. Water regularly, mulch yearly to retain moisture. Divide in spring or autumn, sow fresh seed in spring or late summer. May self-sow for volunteer plants in subsequent seasons.
Features: Good choice for borders, cut flowers. Provides bright color in shady areas of water gardens. Aphid susceptible.

Common name: Goatsbeard
Scientific name: *Aruncus dioicus*
Habitat/Size: Shoreline. Grows to 6 ft. (1.8 m) tall, 4 ft. (1.2 m) wide.
Description: Mounding perennial. Handsome crinkled, tooth-edged leaves below 18 in. (45 cm) stalks. Plumes of drooping, tiny cream-colored flowers. Late spring to early summer blooming.
Plant hardiness: Zones 3–9.
Soil needs: Moist, well-drained, rich in organic matter. Fertility: Rich. 6.0–8.0 pH.
Planting: Full sun to partial shade. 18–24 in. (45–60 cm) apart.
Care: Hardy to 5°F (–15°C). Divide in autumn or spring; plant seeds in autumn.
Features: Good choice for shady nook away from water feature. Cut and dry seed heads for arrangements. North American native.

Common name: Golden-club
Scientific name: *Orontium aquaticum*
Habitat/Size: Shallow-depth marginal, deep-depth marginal. Grows to 14 in. (35 cm) tall.
Description: Deciduous perennial. Metallic blue green, straplike leaves 10 in. (25 cm) long, silvery fuzz above and purplish beneath, angle upward to rise above the surface. Yellow flower clusters, 7 in. (18 cm) wide, top long white stalks, rose red at the base. Spring blooming.
Plant hardiness: Zones 5–10.
Soil needs: Loam. Fertility: Rich. 6.0–8.0 pH.
Planting: Full sun. 2 ft. (60 cm) apart in 1 ft. (30 cm) soil. Submerge 4–18 in. (10–45 cm) deep.
Care: Frost-hardy. Divide in spring or plant fresh seeds in containers.
Features: Good choice for accents in large water feature. North American native.

Common name: Grass, Cotton
Scientific name: *Eriophorum angustifolium*
Habitat/Size: Shoreline, shallow-depth marginal. Grows 6 in. (15 cm) tall, 1 ft. (30 cm) wide.
Description: Perennial, grasslike sedge. Silky, glossy white flower heads highlight this grasslike sedge. April to June blooming.
Plant hardiness: Zones 6–11.
Soil needs: Moist to wet, peaty to clay. Fertility: Average. 6.0 pH.
Planting: Partial shade. 1 ft. (30 cm) apart. Submerge up to 2 in. (50 mm) deep. Plant shoreline plants in containers and bury in soil.
Care: Very frost-hardy. Divide mature clumps, sow seed in spring. Can be very invasive.
Features: Good choice for massing, cut flowers. Provides dancing movement in the garden when silky flowers sway in a slight breeze.

Common name: Hornwort
Scientific name: *Ceratophyllum demersum*
Habitat/Size: Submerged oxygenator. Grows 8–54 in. (20–135 cm) long, depending on size of feature.
Description: Deciduous perennial. Attractive, soft, bright green plumes formed by whorls of tiny brittle leaves on floating stems.
Plant hardiness: Zones 8–11.
Soil needs: Lime-rich water. 7.0–8.0 pH.
Planting: Full sun; tolerates partial shade. Set on water.
Care: Leaves break off and float to bottom of feature. Clean plume debris from bottom of feature to prevent pump and filter clogs.
Features: Foliage provides excellent oxygenation and algae control.

Common name: Horsetail; Scouring Rush
Scientific name: *Equisetum hyemale*
Habitat/Size: Shoreline, shallow-depth marginal. Grows 2–4 ft. (60–120 cm).
Description: Primitive rushlike perennial. Leafless, jointed, hollow green stems bear spikey cones from summer to autumn.
Plant hardiness: Zones 3–11.
Soil needs: Sandy loam. Fertility: Average. 6.5–7.5 pH.
Planting: Full sun in cool climates, partial shade where warmer, sheltered from wind. 2 ft. (60 cm) apart. Submerge 6 in. (15 cm) deep. Can be invasive on shoreline; plant in containers and bury in soil.
Care: Hardy to 22°F (–6°C). Water generously. Remove runners. Divide and root from spring to autumn.
Features: Good choice for natural gardens. An ancient genus, adds a wild primeval look and intriguing vertical pattern.

Common name: Hyssop, Lemon
Scientific name: *Bacopa caroliniana; B. amplexicaulis*
Habitat/Size: Shoreline, shallow-depth marginal. Grows to 2 ft. (60 cm) tall.
Description: Evergreen perennial. Opposite, delicate pale green leaves. Single tiny blue flowers. Leaves are citrus scented when crushed. Summer blooming.
Plant hardiness: Zones 9–11.
Soil needs: Loam enriched with peat moss. Fertility: Average. 6.5–7.0 pH.
Planting: Full sun. Submerge 6 in. (15 cm) deep.
Care: Performs best in warm water. Propagate from cuttings.
Features: Good choice for banks, middle of water features, especially in tropical gardens, among rocks, self-contained water gardens. North American native common to southern pine forests.

IRIS

The vibrant color and stately form of irises are symbolic of a water garden. Their long-stalked, sculptural flowers and swordlike leaves make a handsome backdrop for shorter plants. There are about 60 genera and more than 800 species of irises growing throughout the world. The many genera divide into two categories: those that grow from bulbs and those that grow from rhizomes. The species of iris that grow from rhizomes divide into three categories: crested, bearded, and beardless. Six species of beardless iris and their many cultivars thrive in moist to wet soil or shallow water. It was a beardless water iris, with its three uplifted standards and three graceful falls, that inspired the French *fleur-de-lis* emblem.

Several beardless irises thrive in a water garden environment, including *I. ensata*, Japanese water iris; *I. laevigata*, beardless iris; *I. pseudacorus*, yellow flag iris; and *I. versicolor*, blue flag iris. All grow both in the soil on the shoreline, in above-ground containers, and as shallow-depth marginals, with the rhizomes planted in containers and submerged. Remove rhizomes or their containers from water to overwinter. Plant in odd-numbered groups to add color and stately form to natural style ponds and stream beds. Align them in the soil or in containers to march around the edges of formal pools and watercourses. Plant them in masses for incredible seasonal impact.

Water irises thrive in full sun or light shade and heavy clay soil. Plant iris rhizomes in spring, summer, or autumn for flowers the following year. Group 2 or 3 rhizomes in a 2-in. (50-mm) depression within a 9-in. (23-cm) container or in the ground. Cover with soil, leaving the growing tip exposed. Give a light feeding in early spring and again after blooming. A few irises prefer a dry resting period; move containerized plants out of the water or lift rhizomes and overwinter in damp peat moss.

Once established, they are carefree for several years, when they can be judiciously divided. Divide after blooming by cutting a 2-in. (50-mm) section for each growing tip, discarding the old rhizome and planting the division. Watch for iris sawfly larvae, snail, and slugs, and treat with methods nontoxic to other pond life.

Irises make beautiful, if short-lived, cut flowers. For the longest possible display, cut when buds are opening.

Common name: Iris, Blue Flag
Scientific name: *Iris versicolor*
Habitat/Size: Shoreline, shallow-depth marginal. Grows flower stalks to 30 in. (75 cm) tall.
Description: Tall and vigorous perennial bulb. Narrow, straplike, medium green leaves. Each stem bears 2 or 3 lavender blue or rich violet flowers with white veins. May to July blooming.
Plant hardiness: Zones 4–9.
Soil needs: Wet, clay, rich in organic matter. Fertility: Rich. 5.5–6.5 pH.
Planting: Partial shade. 18 in. (45 cm) apart. Submerge to 6 in. (15 cm) deep.
Care: Very frost-hardy. Keep soil wet. Wear gloves to divide rhizomes or cut stems; juices may irritate skin.
Features: Good choice for accents, cut flowers. Dark brown seed pods add interest to dried arrangements. North American native.

Common name: Lily, Calla
Scientific name: *Zantedeschia aethiopica*
Habitat/Size: Shoreline. Grows 2–4 ft. (60–120 cm) tall.
Description: Elegant tuberous perennial. Stately single white petal encloses a yellow spadix. Flowers and large speckled, arrow-shaped leaves are borne on thick stalks. Spring and autumn blooming.
Plant hardiness: Zones 8–11.
Soil needs: Moist to wet, sandy to clay loam. Fertility: Average. 6.0–8.0 pH.
Planting: Partial shade. Clumps 16 in. (40 cm) apart.
Care: Plant rhizomes 4 in. (10 cm) deep. Remove faded flowers. Reduce water after blooming, with a dry resting period after leaves die back. Mulch at northern limits. In cold winter zones, pull up rhizomes and overwinter. Potted plants bloom best when root bound.
Features: Good choice for shaded shoreline of streams, in above-ground containers along watercourses, cut flowers. For surprising color, try 'Pink Giant', 'Green Goddess', or 'Yellow Mammoth'.

Common name: Lily, Kaffir
Scientific name: *Clivia miniata*
Habitat/Size: Shoreline. Grows to 2 ft. (60 cm) tall.
Description: Tall, stately, richly colored perennial herb with bulblike tuberous roots. Broad, waxy, dark green leaves 2 in. (50 mm) wide and 18 in. (45 cm) long. Funnel-shaped flowers 3 in. (75 mm) long, deep red orange, yellow centers. Early spring blooming.
Plant hardiness: Zones 9–11.
Soil needs: Loam, moist, well-drained. Fertility: Rich. 7.0 pH.
Planting: Partial shade. 6–12 in. (15–30 cm) apart. Plant tuberous roots just below the soil surface.
Care: Keep soil moist. Feed with liquid fertilizer through the growing season.
Features: Good choice for containers, massing in shade areas around water feature. Attracts hummingbirds. Allow flowers to form seed heads for interesting late spring texture in the garden.

Common name: Lily-of-the-Nile; African Lily
Scientific name: *Agapanthus orientalis*
Habitat/Size: Shoreline. Grows 18–48 in. (45–120 cm) tall. Colonies may reach 3 ft. (90 cm) in diameter if undivided.
Description: Perennial bulbs produce arching foliage and upright flower stems. Very long, straplike succulent leaves. Stalks bear dense clusters of as many as 100 purple or white tube-shaped flowers. Summer blooming.
Plant hardiness: Zones 8–11.
Soil needs: Moist, well-drained. Fertility: Average. 6.0–7.0 pH.
Planting: Full sun to partial shade. 1–2 ft. (30–60 cm) apart.
Care: Easy. Water moderately. Feed with liquid fertilizer. Propagate from seeds, division in autumn or spring.
Features: Good choice for accents, containers, massing. Long-lasting blooms. Evergreen in mild climates. Mealybug susceptible.

PLANTAIN LILY

There are as many as 40 species of plants known scientifically as *Hosta* and by the common names plantain lily and daylily. All are herbaceous perennials that grow from a small rhizome. Mostly native to Japan, and some to Korea and China, their beautiful foliage and interesting texture have come to visually define water gardens throughout the world. They bring fascinating form and color to a cool, shaded garden. The lush mounds of big leaves often outshine the flowers. Popular plantain lilies serve many uses in the garden. They make an ideal choice on the shady shoreline surrounding a water feature where they provide interesting texture, frame garden accessories, and serve as shelter for birds and amphibians. Plantain lilies also make an excellent visual bridge between the feature and the remainder of the garden. Leaf colors include shimmering blues to emerald greens, yellows, cream and white. Textures range from crinkled quilting to pleating to swirled ribbing, with forms from strap-shaped to heart-shaped. Slender stems of small lilylike flowers bloom above the foliage for several weeks from summer and into autumn.

Hundreds of cultivars have been developed from popular species, including waxy-leafed *H. undulata* and smooth-leafed *H. sieboldiana*. Generally, they are hardy from USDA plant hardiness zones 6–10, and some to zone 3. The many different types have different sun and shade requirements. Those with blue leaves need cool shade, away from direct sun, to keep their color. Solid greens need filtered shade; yellows and golds nearly full sun; and variegated types, a balance of shade and sun to maintain vibrant colors through summer.

All plantain lilies do best in moist, well-drained soil rich in organic matter. Generous watering helps any plantain lily handle more sun, which encourages blooming, but soggy soil, especially during winter dormancy, can lead to crown rot. They need protection from strong wind and from slugs, snails, and deer that savor the tasty leaves. Once established, they're carefree, with division only every 3–5 years. They become dormant with the first frosts, and in spring emerge with a fresh display.

Common name: Lily, Plantain
Scientific name: *Hosta Sieboldiana*
Habitat/Size: Shoreline. Grows 2–3 ft. (60–90 cm) tall.
Description: Perennial. Extravagant pointed leaves—gray green to bluish, to 14 in. (35 cm) long and wide—form a dense clump. In autumn, they turn a warm golden brown. Small purple white blossoms bloom low above the foliage. Spring to early summer blooming.
Plant hardiness: Zones 6–10.
Soil needs: Moist, well-drained, clay to sand. Fertility: Average. 6.0–7.0 pH.
Planting: Partial shade for best foliage, full sun for best blooms. 2–4 ft. (60–120 cm) apart.
Care: Divide mature clumps when growth starts, or in autumn where soil stays moist. Slug, snail susceptible, especially during new growth from spring to early summer.
Features: Good choice for accents, massing along water's edge.

Common name: Lily, Toad
Scientific name: *Tricyrtis* species
Habitat/Size: Shoreline. Grows 2–3 ft. (60–90 cm).
Description: Nearly 15 species of rhizomatous perennials. Alternate, broadly oval, shiny, dark green leaves. Single or double clusters of small, unusually shaped, spotted yellow, white, purple flowers 1 in. (25 mm) wide. Summer to autumn blooming.
Plant hardiness: Zones 4–9.
Soil needs: Well-drained, rich in organic matter. Fertility: Rich. 5.0 pH.
Planting: Partial shade. 18–24 in. (45–60 cm) apart.
Care: Water regularly. In colder areas, dig up the rhizomes and store indoors in winter. Propagate from seeds, division.
Features: Good choice along paths and entrance to water feature, containers, shade gardens. Long lived.

Common name: Lilyturf
Scientific name: *Liriope* species
Habitat/Size: Shoreline. Grows 8–24 in. (20–60 cm).
Description: About five species of evergreen perennials. Attractive, grasslike, glossy green, sometimes variegated with white, evergreen leaves, up to 2 ft. (60 cm) long. Dense clusters of 4–7 small purple or white flowers on drooping stalks. Summer blooming.
Plant hardiness: Zones 6–10.
Soil needs: Well-drained. Fertility: Average to rich. 7.0 pH.
Planting: Partial sun to full shade. 8–12 in. (20–30 cm) apart.
Care: Very easy. Water regularly but moderately. Can be invasive in warm-winter areas. Slug, snail susceptible. Propagate from division of offsets in early spring.
Features: Good choice for borders, edgings, ground cover.

Common name: Lizard's-tail; Water-dragon; Swamp Lily
Scientific name: *Saururus cernuus*
Habitat/Size: Shallow-depth marginal. Grows 3¼–5 ft. (1–1.5 m) long from aromatic rhizome. Broad, palmlike leaves to 6 in. (15 cm) long.
Description: Creeping deciduous perennial. Sweetly aromatic, heart-shaped, bright green leaves rise above the surface on red stems, bear a soft down when young. Impressively long, pipe cleanerlike, creamy white fragrant flower tails 4–6 in. (10–15 cm) long, curl at the tips.
Plant hardiness: Zones 4–9.
Soil needs: Wet. Fertility: Average. 6.0–8.0 pH.
Planting: Full sun to partial shade. 8 in. (20 cm) apart. Submerge 2–6 in. (50–150 mm) deep.
Care: Divide regularly for strongest growth. Root cuttings or sow ripe seed in containers.
Features: Good choice for massing at water's edge, shade garden. Flowers in dense shade. Grown mainly for distinctive foliage. Eastern North American native.

LOTUS

The ultimate flowering plant for a still-water feature, the lotus raises a jungle of huge leaves and waxy, fragrant flowers followed by decorative seedpods. Buddhists contemplating its beauty emerging from muddy depths see in the lotus a symbol of sacred perfection.

Known scientifically as *Nelumbo* species, lotuses are native to the tropics. In a natural environment, they thrive in 8 ft. (2.4 m) of warm water and reach an astonishing size. In temperate gardens, shallow water helps maintain the warmth they need for flowering—3–4 weeks at 80°F (27°C). Most new plants bloom in their second year. Where frost occurs, the tubers of all but a few cultivars must be lifted and overwintered. Replanted in early spring, they grow phenomenally, reaching full blooming size by summer. Once the leaves go aerial—rise above the surface like umbrellas—flowers will soon appear.

There are many cultivars to choose from—day and night bloomers in colors ranging from white to deep red, jade green to sky blue and deep purple. Miniatures such as 'Mono Botan' and 'Ben Gibson' suit a small feature.

The lotus's brittle, fragile tuber needs careful handling and plenty of room to spread its roots. Choose a large, strong plastic container as the roots can be very invasive. Plant when root and leaf growth just begin in spring; lay the tuber horizontally, 2 in. (50 mm) deep in the container of soil. The growing tip always must be exposed to the water—even after adding a top layer of gravel. At first, allow only 2 in. (50 mm) water to cover; after growth starts, gradually increase to 4–6 in. (10–15 cm), to a final placement of 2 ft. (60 cm). Fertilize at planting and twice monthly thereafter. Overwinter by gently lifting, washing, and storing the tuber in moist sand. Carefully divide large tubers when replanting in spring. Otherwise, leave the roots undisturbed.

The glorious flowers last just 3 days, with fragrance on the first day only. When cutting for arrangements, include about 1 ft. (30 cm) of stalk, and quickly support it in a tall, narrow vase with deep water. Allow some of the flower centers to turn to seedpods on the plant, harvesting them when brown; they make wonderful accents for fresh or dried arrangements.

Common name: Lotus, American; Water Chinquapin
Scientific name: *Nelumbo lutea*
Habitat/Size: Deep-water submersible. Grows 2½–5 ft. (75–150 cm) tall.
Description: Deciduous perennial. Single white, cream, yellow blossoms, 7–11 in. (18–28 cm) across, are held 10 in. (25 cm) above wide green leaves 12–18 in. (30–45 cm) in diameter. Midsummer to autumn blooming.
Plant hardiness: Zones 8–11; zones 4–7 with winter protection.
Soil needs: Loam or clay loam, rich in organic matter. Fertility: Rich. 6.0–8.0 pH.
Planting: Full sun. 5 ft. (1.5 m) apart. Submerge to 18 in. (45 cm) over crown. Propagate from divison of rhizomes or sow scarified seeds in shallow containers.
Care: In cold climates, remove from water in winter.
Features: Good choice for accent in still pools, ponds. North American native. Grows wild east of the Mississippi River. Native Americans harvested the seeds and tubers as an important food source.

Common name: Mallow, Rose; Swamp Hibiscus
Scientific name: *Hibiscus Moscheutos*
Habitat/Size: Shoreline. Grows to 8 ft. (2.4 m) tall, 3–5 ft. (90–150 cm) wide.
Description: Perennial. Maplelike toothed leaves on tall, sturdy stems bear single white, pink, red flowers, 4–8 in. (10–20 cm) wide. Late summer to early autumn blooming.
Plant hardiness: Zones 5–9.
Soil needs: Moist, well-drained, rich in organic matter. Fertility: Rich. 6.0–8.0 pH.
Planting: Partial sun, tolerates full sun, sheltered from wind. 5 ft. (1.5 m) apart.
Care: Hardy to 23°F (–5°C). From seed to flowering takes 4–5 months. Seeds germinate best if soaked overnight before planting. Feed every 1–2 months during growth. After flowering, prune long shoots. Mulch roots in winter, or remove and store.
Features: Good choice for hedge, screen. Shorter cultivars bear flowers up to 10 in. (25 cm) across. 'Southern Belle' is most common garden variety. 'Disco Belle' grows 18–24 in. (45–60 cm).

Common name: Manna Grass, Variegated
Scientific name: *Glyceria maxima* 'Variegata'
Habitat/Size: Shoreline, shallow-depth marginal. Grows to 3 ft. (90 cm) tall.
Description: Deciduous grass. Gracefully arching foliage, pinkish when new, turns striped cream, yellow, green. Creamy, purple-tinged flowers. Midsummer blooming.
Plant hardiness: Zones 5–10.
Soil needs: Moist to wet, clay, rich in organic matter. Fertility: Rich. 6.0–8.0 pH.
Planting: Full sun. 15 in. (38 cm) apart. Submerge up to 6 in. (15 cm) deep.
Care: Can be invasive on shoreline. Remove new runners. Grow from seed or division.
Features: Good choice for accent, border, filler. Heavy clay soil helps curb invasive growth.

Common name: Maple, Japanese
Scientific name: *Acer palmatum*
Habitat/Size: Shoreline. Grows 15–20 ft. (4.5–6 m) tall.
Description: Deciduous tree or shrub. Light green, toothed leaves, deeply cut into 5–9 lobes, 2–4 in. (5–10 cm) long; spring growth is red, turning scarlet or yellow in autumn. Inconspicuous flowers. Spectacularly beautiful branching habit.
Plant hardiness: Zones 5–9.
Soil needs: Moist, well-drained. Fertility: Average to rich. 6.5 pH.
Planting: Full sun to partial shade. Space according to desired effect.
Care: Water deeply, moderately. Protect from wind; hot sun in zones 8–9.
Features: Good choice for accents, back of water garden. Provides year-round interest: Red leaf growth in early spring, tiny white flowers in midspring, green leaves in summer, crimson autumn foliage, stark branches in winter.

Common name: Marsh Marigold
Scientific name: *Caltha palustris*
Habitat/Size: Shoreline, shallow-depth marginal. Grows to 2 ft. (60 cm) tall.
Description: Deciduous perennial. Profusion of yellow flowers, 2 in (50 mm) wide. Early spring blooming. Glossy, leathery leaves follow. Dormant in summer.
Plant hardiness: Zones 3–8.
Soil needs: Deep, rich in organic matter. Fertility: Rich. 6–8 pH.
Planting: Full sun to full shade. 6 in. (15 cm) apart in clusters 2–3 ft. (60–90 cm) apart. Submerge up to 6 in. (15 cm) deep.
Care: Extremely frost-hardy. Fertilize established plants in spring. Keep moist through summer, mulching yearly to conserve moisture. Divide in spring; sow fresh seed, kept moist, in late summer.
Features: Good choice for very early blooms. May self-sow. North American native.

Common name: Masterwort
Scientific name: *Astrantia major*
Habitat/Size: Shoreline. Grows 2–3 ft. (60–90 cm) tall.
Description: Perennial. Palm-shaped, sometimes variegated leaves. Colorful, showy, creamy white flowers 2–3 in. (50–75 mm) wide, are tinged pink by a collar of purple braces below the petals. Spring blooming.
Plant hardiness: Zones 5–7.
Soil needs: Well-drained, moist. Fertility: Average. 7.0 pH.
Planting: Full sun to partial shade. 18 in. (45 cm) apart. Plant in autumn or early spring.
Care: Water frequently. Propagate from seeds in autumn, division in autumn or spring.
Features: Good choice for background, colorful screen around garden ponds and along streams.

Common name: Meadow Sweet; Spiraea
Scientific name: *Astilbe* species
Habitat/Size: Shoreline. Grows 6–48 in. (15–120 cm) tall, 2–3 ft. (60–90 cm) wide.
Description: Perennial. Dense clumps of fresh green, finely divided leaves, sometimes coppery when young, spread from branching rhizomes. Feathery white, pink, dark red flowers. Early summer blooming.
Plant hardiness: Zones 7–10.
Soil needs: Moist, well-drained, sandy, rich in organic matter. Fertility: Average. 5.5–7.0 pH.
Planting: Full sun to full shade in warmest zones. Spacing varies by species.
Care: In hot summers may need constant watering. Cut to ground level in late winter. Mulch yearly with organic matter. Divide clumps every 3–4 years in spring.
Features: Good choice for cool climates, cut flowers, dried arrangements. Most nursery plants are *A.* x *arendsii* hybrids.

Common name: Melon Sword; Texas Mudbaby
Scientific name: *Echinodorus cordifolius*
Habitat/Size: Deep-depth marginal, deep-water submersible. Grows 8–24 in. (20–60 cm) tall.
Description: Perennial. Spear-shaped or oval leaves grow on slender stems from a central clump. Submerged plants eventually send out emergent leaves, then produce white flowers.
Plant hardiness: Zones 5–11.
Soil needs: Wet, rich in organic matter. Water 59–86°F (15–30°C). Fertility: Rich. 5.0–8.0 pH.
Planting: Partial to full shade. 1 ft. (30 cm) apart. Submerge 6–20 in. (15–50 cm) deep.
Care: Easy. Fast-growing. Prune to control growth. May self-sow.
Features: Leaves will be paler with less light. 'Ovalis' is easiest for beginners. 'Tropica Marble Queen' needs more acidic water, but features handsome yellow-and-green marbled leaves. North American native.

Common name: Mint, Water
Scientific name: *Mentha aquatica*
Habitat/Size: Shoreline, shallow-depth marginal. Grows to 3 ft. (90 cm) tall.
Description: Spreading perennial. Bushy clumps of aromatic, fuzzy, tooth-edged leaves bear small round heads of lilac blue flowers. Late summer to early autumn blooming.
Plant hardiness: Zones 6–10.
Soil needs: Moist to wet, clay. Fertility: Average. 6.0–8.0 pH.
Planting: Full sun to partial shade. 1 ft. (30 cm) apart. Submerge to 6 in. (15 cm) deep.
Care: Easy. Plant seed in early spring, root divisions or cuttings in spring or autumn. Pinch back to keep bushy. Plant in containers and bury to control growth. Can become weedy.
Features: Good choice for stream banks, around seating areas. Edible. Sunny site produces strongest fragrance. Fast growing. Attracts butterflies.

Common name: Monkey Flower
Scientific name: *Mimulus cardinalis*
Habitat/Size: Shoreline. Grows 1–4 ft. (30–120 cm) tall.
Description: Perennial. Crinkled, serrated, sticky leaves grow in pairs. Tubular scarlet, orange, yellow blossoms. April to October blooming.
Plant hardiness: Zones 6–11.
Soil needs: Wet, rich in organic matter. Fertility: Rich. 6.0–8.0 pH.
Planting: Full sun to partial shade. Shelter from wind. 2 ft. (60 cm) apart.
Care: Plant after all frost danger is past. Feed liquid fertilizer monthly during growing season. Trim rhizomes to control growth.
Features: Good choice for edges of ponds and streams. Western U.S. native. Attracts hummingbirds.

Common name: Moss, Fairy; Mosquito Fern; Mosquito Plant
Scientific name: *Azolla caroliniana*
Habitat/Size: Surface floater.
Description: Small, drifting aquatic deciduous ferns spread quickly, covering water surface with attractive soft, pea green leaves. In autumn they turn pink, bronze, red as they go dormant. Resting buds submerge through winter frosts. May take root in a muddy bottom.
Plant hardiness: Zones 8–11.
Soil needs: 6.0–8.0 pH.
Planting: One cutting can colonize a pond.
Care: Naturalizes quickly. In warm zones, can be very invasive. Clean fallen buds from bottom of feature to prevent pump and filter clogs.
Features: Good choice for colorful accent. Eastern U.S. and Caribbean native.

Common name: Orchid, Stream
Scientific name: *Epipactis gigantea*
Habitat/Size: Shoreline. Grows to 3 ft. (90 cm) tall.
Description: Terrestrial orchid. Lancelike leaves to 8 in. (20 cm) long. Strongly veined pink to rose flowers 1 in. (25 mm) wide. Summer blooming.
Plant hardiness: Zones 9–10.
Soil needs: Well-drained, fibrous loam with sharp sand and leaf mold. Fertility: Rich. 6.0–6.5 pH.
Planting: Full sun. 2–3 ft. (60–90 cm) apart.
Care: Growing conditions must be met for plant to thrive. Keep moist. Propagate by seed, division, cuttings. Plant in containers and bury in soil to establish and maintain rich soil needs.
Features: Good choice for accents, along shoreline of streams in warm conditions, greenhouses. Western North American native.

Common name: Palm, Umbrella
Scientific name: *Cyperus alternifolius*
Habitat/Size: Shoreline. Grows 2–4 ft. (60–120 cm) tall.
Description: Robust perennial. Exotic vertical form. Stiff, narrow leaves fan out in umbrella shapes atop tall stems.
Plant hardiness: Zones 10–11.
Soil needs: Rich in organic matter. Fertility: Rich. 6.0–8.0 pH.
Planting: Partial shade, humid. 3 ft. (90 cm) apart.
Care: Plant seeds, divide rhizomes, or root cuttings from flower heads in spring. Keep well watered. When clumps grow too large, divide and replant smaller outer sections, discarding old centers. Prune spent stems. Remove seed heads to prevent self-sowing.
Features: Good choice for tropical gardens. Dwarf cultivars 'Gracilis' and 'Nanus' suit small-space gardens. Related to papyrus used by ancient people for paper.

Common name: Papyrus, Dwarf
Scientific name: *Cyperus isocladus*
Habitat/Size: Shoreline, shallow-depth marginal. Grows to 18 in. (45 cm) tall.
Description: Perennial. Smaller version of papyrus cultivated since ancient times. Perennial, delicate, leafless stems bear airy starbursts of fine branching leaves and up to 100 tiny brown flowers.
Plant hardiness: Zones 8–11.
Soil needs: Moist to wet. Fertility: Average. 6.0–8.0 pH.
Planting: Full sun to partial shade. 1 ft. (30 cm) apart. Submerge 1–2 in. (25–50 mm) over crown. Can be invasive on shoreline; plant in containers and bury in soil. Propagate from divisions or tubers or sow seeds in spring or autumn.
Care: Can be somewhat invasive.
Features: Good choice for accents, large above-ground containers placed along a watercourse, oasis-style streams, small-space gardens.

Common name: Parrotleaf; Alligator Weed
Scientific name: *Alternanthera ficoidea*
Habitat/Size: Shoreline. Grows 6–15 in. (15–38 cm) tall.
Description: Tender perennial herb. Grown for foliage. Vibrantly color-splashed and veined leaves on creeping stems form a low mat.
Plant hardiness: Zones 8–11.
Soil needs: Moisture-retentive, well-drained, rich in organic matter. Fertility: Rich. 6.0–8.0 pH.
Planting: Full sun to partial shade. 4–10 in. (10–25 cm) apart.
Care: Fast-growing, drought-tolerant. Root cuttings in spring, divide, grow from seed.
Features: Good choice for ground cover around water feature edgings, can be clipped to height. Warm climates provide the richest color.

Common name: Parrot's-feather
Scientific name: *Myriophyllum aquaticum*
Habitat/Size: Shallow-depth marginal. Grows stems to 6 ft. (1.8 m) long.
Description: Deciduous perennial. Trailing form. Submerged foliage is chartreuse, fine, feathery. Emerging stems bear whorls of narrow blue green leaves. Tiny, bright yellow green flowers. Summer blooming.
Plant hardiness: Zones 6–11.
Soil needs: Sandy, rich in organic matter. Fertility: Rich. 5.5–9.0 pH.
Planting: Full sun to partial shade. Clusters 6 in. (15 cm) apart. Submerge 6 in. (15 cm) deep.
Care: Trim to allow light to reach submerged stems. Can be somewhat invasive. Control excess growth by cutting back and thinning. Cuttings root readily.
Features: Good choice for casual ponds, streams. Stems trail from water to shoreline. South American native, naturalized in southeastern U.S.

Common name: Pennywort, Water
Scientific name: *Hydrocotyle verticillata*
Habitat/Size: Shoreline. Grows 2–6 in. (50–150 mm) tall, 2 in. (50 mm) wide. Spreads 1–5 ft. (30–150 cm).
Description: Perennial. Produces masses of fresh green, nasturtiumlike leaves, trailing from bank to water. Small white or greenish flowers. Late summer blooming.
Plant hardiness: Zones 9–11.
Soil needs: Constantly moist. Water 41–77°F (5–25°C). Fertility: Average. 6.0–7.0 pH.
Planting: Full sun to full shade, 4 in. (10 cm) apart.
Care: Plant seeds or divisions.
Features: Good choice for ground cover very close to water's edge. Charming and versatile, it grows from shoreline to water.

Common name: Phlox
Scientific name: *Phlox paniculata*
Habitat/Size: Grows 1–2 ft. (30–60 cm) tall, 2 ft. (60 cm) wide.
Description: Clumping perennial. Thin, veiny, lance-shaped, dense, dark green leaves 3–6 in. (75–150 mm) long. Pyramid-shaped clusters 10–14 in. (25–35 cm) wide, of small, white, pink, red, lavender, or blue flowers. Spring to summer blooming.
Plant hardiness: Zones 3–10.
Soil needs: Moist, well-drained. Fertility: Rich. 7.0 pH.
Planting: Full sun to partial shade. 18 in. (45 cm) apart.
Care: Moderately difficult. Water frequently. Fertilize regularly. Stake for support. Propagate from seeds, division, cuttings.
Features: Good choice for borders, as transition from water feature to other areas of the garden. Some slightly scented. North American native. Powdery mildew, rust, spider mite susceptible.

Common name: Pickerel Weed; Blue Pickerel Rush
Scientific name: *Pontederia cordata*
Habitat/Size: Shallow-depth marginal, deep-depth marginal. Grows 2–4 ft. (60–120 cm) tall.
Description: Perennial. A profusion of large, erect, translucent arrow-shaped leaves rises well above the water surface. Spikes of blue violet flowers, 6 in. (15 cm) wide, each with a yellow dot on the upper petal. July to September blooming.
Plant hardiness: Zones 3–11.
Soil needs: Moist to wet, sandy or clay loam. Fertility: Average. 6.0–8.0 pH.
Planting: Full sun to partial shade in warm climates. 4 ft. (1.2 m) apart. Submerge 1–12 in. (25–300 mm) over crown.
Care: Easy. Plant from early spring to late summer. Deadhead after bloom to encourage blooming.
Features: Good choice for adding color throughout the growing season. Attracts dragonflies. Long blooming. Goes dormant in winter. North American native.

Common name: Pitcher Plant
Scientific name: *Sarracenia* species
Habitat/Size: Shoreline. Grows 5–25 in. (13–63 cm) tall.
Description: Eight species of rhizomatous, carnivorous perennials. Unique spotted and striped pitchers stand erect or sprawl in a rosette. Pink, coral, red, greenish yellow blossoms.
Plant hardiness: Zones 7–11.
Soil needs: Moist, coarse mix of sand and peat, high in organic matter. Fertility: Average. 6.0 pH.
Planting: Full sun at least 5 hours per day, high humidity; low-mineral, nonalkaline water.
Care: Grow by seed or division, March–September. Keep very wet when growing, cool and moist in winter. Avoid spraying water directly on foliage. Cut spent leaves to 1 in. (25 mm) at the base.
Features: Spots and stripes attract insects, which slide down the slippery inner walls and drown in collected rainwater. Eastern North American native. Endangered in some regions, choose only cultivated specimens.

Common name: Pondweed, Canadian; Waterweed
Scientific name: *Elodea canadensis*
Habitat/Size: Submerged oxygenator, deep-depth marginal. Grows to 12 ft. (3.6 m) long.
Description: A classic water garden plant, with long undulating stems of translucent, bright green whorled leaves. Purplish white flowers. July to September blooming.
Plant hardiness: Zones 3–9.
Soil needs: Loam. Cold water. Fertility: Average. 8.0 pH.
Planting: Full sun. Clusters every 2 sq. ft. (0.19 m²) of water surface, several to a container. Submerge 1 ft. (30 cm).
Care: Easy. Fast growing, can be somewhat invasive. Needs water movement to pollinate. In spring, toss cuttings into water or plant in containers.
Features: Good choice for fish ponds. North American native.

Common name: Primrose
Scientific name: *Primula japonica*
Habitat/Size: Shoreline. Grows 6–30 in. (15–75 cm) tall, 6–12 in. (15–30 cm) wide.
Description: Clumping herbaceous perennial. Showy, large, coarse, cabbagelike pale green leaves. Sturdy tall spikes of red, pink, or white flowers. April to June blooming.
Plant hardiness: Zones 5–8.
Soil needs: Moist. Avoid soggy. Fertility: Average to poor. 6.0 pH.
Planting: Full sun to partial shade.
Care: Hardy. Propagate from seeds, division.
Features: Good choce for edges, ground cover. Long succession of blooms. Will self-sow. Future plants may produce different bloom colors.

Common name: Queen-of-the-Prairie; Meadowsweet
Scientific name: *Filipendula rubra*
Habitat/Size: Shoreline. Grows to 7½ ft. (2.3 m) tall, 3 ft. (90 cm) wide.
Description: Perennial. Mounds of dense, deeply cut leaves stay fresh well into autumn. Large clusters of tiny peachy pink flowers bloom on tall stems. Mid-summer and autumn blooming.
Plant hardiness: Zones 3–9.
Soil needs: Moist to wet, rich in organic matter. Fertility: Rich. 6.0–8.0 pH.
Planting: Full sun to partial shade. 3 ft. (90 cm) apart.
Care: Frost-hardy. Plant seeds in autumn or spring. Mulch in spring. In regions of lengthy frost, protect roots with bracken or branches. Divide in autumn or winter. Powdery mildew susceptible.
Features: Good choice for background. Long-lived. Endangered in some regions, choose only cultivated specimens.

Common name: Reed, Common
Scientific name: *Phragmites australis*
Habitat/Size: Shoreline. Grows stems to 11 ft. (3.3 m) tall, leaves to 2 ft. (60 cm) wide.
Description: Deciduous perennial. Decorative, tall, dense stands of rough grassy blades with pampaslike, feathery flower plumes. July to September blooming. Tawny, to purple, turns russet gold in autumn.
Plant hardiness: Zones 5–11.
Soil needs: Moist, deep. Fertility: Average. 6.0–8.0 pH.
Planting: Full sun. 4 ft. (1.2 m) apart.
Care: Hardy. Can be very invasive. Plant in containers buried in soil to control growth. Divide established clumps.
Features: Good choice for background, screen. Reeds harvested to make lattice. The dwarf 'Humilis' is a good choice for small-space gardens. 'Rubra' flower heads blush crimson. 'Variegatus' leaves are green striped with bright yellow.

Common name: Rhubarb, Giant Ornamental
Scientific name: *Gunnera manicata*
Habitat/Size: Shoreline. Grows to 8 ft. (2.4 m) high and wide.
Description: Perennial. Impressive in size and form, its huge, rough-surfaced, prickly-bottomed leaves fan out from thick, thorny stalks. Intriguing, conical russet green flower heads, up to 3 ft. (90 cm) tall. Summer blooming.
Plant hardiness: Zones 7–9.
Soil needs: Moist, porous, rich in organic matter. Fertility: Rich. 6.0–8.0 pH.
Planting: Partial shade. Sheltered from wind. 8 ft. (2.4 m) apart.
Care: Seeds may germinate poorly. Mulch young plants in winter. Clear spent leaves and stems, use for frost protection.
Features: Good choice for back of garden away from water feature, accent, screen. *G. tinctoria* is similar but smaller, a good choice for small-space gardens. Avoid planting near paths or to shield equipment due to thorny stalks.

Common name: Ribbon Grass; Gardener's-garters; Reed Canary Grass
Scientific name: *Phalaris arundinacea*
Habitat/Size: Shoreline. Grows to 4 ft. (1.2 m) tall, 2 ft. (60 cm) wide.
Description: Tall, rhizomatous, perennial grass. Narrow, brightly variegated blades bear stalks of tiny purplish green spikelets. Available in white, pink-tinged variegations. Summer to autumn blooming.
Plant hardiness: Zones 4–10.
Soil needs: Moist, well-drained. Fertility: Poor. 6.0–8.0 pH.
Planting: Full sun for best color. 2 ft. (60 cm) apart.
Care: Frost-hardy. Can be somewhat invasive. To confine spread, plant in containers and bury in soil. Divide established clumps. Shear sun-scorched growth in summer, prune in spring.
Features: Good choice for high ground cover to fill in gaps. Long lived.

Common name: Rodgersia
Scientific name: *Rodgersia* species
Habitat/Size: Shoreline. Grows 3–6 ft. (90–180 cm) tall, depending on species.
Description: About five species of rhizomatous perennials. Young leaves bear soft felt, turning bronze when mature. Airy canopies of white to rose flowers rise above open fan of big handsome leaflets in summer, turning to attractive seed heads in autumn.
Plant hardiness: Zones 4–9.
Soil needs: Well-drained, rich in organic matter. Fertility: Rich. 6.0–8.0 pH.
Planting: Full sun to full shade, sheltered from wind. 30 in. (75 cm) apart.
Care: Keep soil constantly moist, especially in drought; leaves may scorch in hot sun. Mulch yearly. Grow from seed or divide clumps in early spring. Spreads by branching rhizomes that form a mass over time.
Features: Good choice for accents, massing.

Common name: Rush, Flowering
Scientific name: *Butomus umbellatus*
Habitat/Size: Shallow-depth marginal, deep-depth marginal. Grows to 5 ft. (1.5 m) tall, 4 ft. (1.2 m) wide.
Description: Perennial. Bold, imposing, grassy rush produces branched clusters of pale pink flowers, sometime half-hidden among its twisted, razor-edged leaf blades. Young leaves turn from purplish bronze to green. Summer blooming.
Plant hardiness: Zones 4–9.
Soil needs: Clay loam. Fertility: Average. 6.0–8.0 pH.
Planting: Full sun to partial shade. 4 ft. (1.2 m) apart. Submerge to 10 in. (25 cm) deep.
Care: For best summer flowering, divide and replant yearly in spring. Plant seed spring or summer. Keep fresh seed moist, sow in sand in containers, submerge in pots of water. Once seedlings sprout, plant in containers and submerge with ½ in. (13 mm) water over surface; lower as foliage grows.
Features: Good choice for accents, border. Leaves are sharp; plant away from footpaths.

Common name: Rush, Giant Variegated Mediterranean
Scientific name: *Arundo Donax* 'Variegata'
Habitat/Size: Shoreline. Grows to 18 ft. (5.4 m) tall.
Description: Large perennial grass. Bamboolike, reedy stems arch gracefully outward, clothed in drooping leaf blades 2 ft. (60 cm) long. Narrow flower heads reach to 2 ft. (60 cm), first rose-tinged, fading later to gray white. Summer blooming.
Plant hardiness: Zones 9–11.
Soil needs: Moist, well-drained, rich in organic matter. Fertility: Rich. 6.0–8.0 pH.
Planting: Full sun to partial shade, sheltered from wind. 9 ft. (2.7 m) apart.
Care: Species tolerates 23°F (-5°C), but varieties are more tender. Tolerates soggy soil. For best foliage, cut stems down to the base in late autumn.
Features: Good choice for accents, screens. Use branching seed heads in dried arrangement. Invasive in native tropics and subtropics.

Common name: Rush, Soft; Corkscrew Rush
Scientific name: *Juncus effusus*
Habitat/Size: Shoreline. Grows 2–4 ft. (60–120 cm) tall, 2 ft. (60 cm) wide.
Description: Perennial grass. Dense sprays of round, leafless stems bear tiny flower clusters below the tips.
Plant hardiness: Zones 4–10.
Soil needs: Wet, clay. Fertility: Poor. 6.0 pH.
Planting: Best in partial shade, tolerates full sun. 2 ft. (60 cm) apart.
Care: Easy in ideal conditions. Divide established clumps in spring. Can be invasive on shoreline; plant in containers and bury in soil.
Features: Good choice for large pond, natural garden accents, cover for birds. Often grown in above-ground containers. Can be placed along watercourses for interesting effect. Intensely grown in Japan. This is the traditional rush for rush mats and rush candles.

Common name: Rush, Variegated
Scientific name: *Baumea rubiginosa* 'Variegata'
Habitat/Size: Shoreline. Grows 1–2 ft. (30–60 cm) tall.
Description: Evergreen. Forms mass of stiffly upright, swordlike leaf blades. Bright yellow stripe edges one side of each glossy green blade, creating a variegated pattern of leaf color.
Plant hardiness: Zones 8–11.
Soil needs: Moist, not soggy. Fertility: Average. 6.0–8.0 pH.
Planting: Full sun to partial shade. 1 ft. (30 cm) apart.
Care: Thrives in loose soil with frequent watering. Divide clumps in spring.
Features: Good choice for edges of streams, creating interesting texture in shoreline plantings. Maintains fresh, neat appearance, spreading slowly. Excellent angular contrast with round or ferny foliage.

Common name: Sedge
Scientific name: *Carex* species
Habitat/Size: Shoreline. Size varies by species.
Description: About 2000 species of rhizomatous perennial grasslike plants forming distinctive clumps and mats. Many offer variegated, colorful foliage.
Plant hardiness: Zones 3–9.
Soil needs: Moist to wet. Fertility: Average. 6.0–8.0 pH.
Planting: Full sun to full shade. Spacing varies by species. Sow seeds in autumn.
Care: Hardy. Divide in spring, grow from ripe seed. Found worldwide in temperate and subarctic bogs, moors. Vast, varied group has wide-ranging requirements. Some tend to be invasive.
Features: Good choice for ground covers, containers, edgings, erosion control, houseplant. Available in many variegated colors and textures. Waterside clumps make appealing reflections. Provides forage and shelter for wildlife.

Common name: Skunk Cabbage
Scientific name: *Lysichiton americanum*
Habitat/Size: Shoreline. Grows 3–6 ft. (90–180 cm) tall.
Description: Deciduous perennial. Lush leaves, 4 ft. (1.2 m) wide, unfurl after blooming, with slight musky odor. Yellow flowerlike spathes enclose a spadix of tiny greenish flowers. Late winter to early spring blooming.
Plant hardiness: Zones 5–9.
Soil needs: Damp to wet, deep, loam, rich in organic matter. Fertility: Rich. 6.0–8.0 pH.
Planting: Full sun to partial shade. Cool, moist climates. 4 ft. (1.2 m) apart.
Care: Plant 2–3-year-old plants; those grown from seed may take 6 years to bloom. Divide young plants. May self-sow.
Features: Good choice for natural, lighted gardens. When backlit, the juicy leaves glow like stained glass. Slow growing. North American native.

Common name: Snowdrop
Scientific name: *Leucojum aestivum*
Habitat/Size: Shoreline. Grows 11–15 in. (28–38 cm) tall.
Description: Bulbs form grassy clumps of deep green leaf blades. Dainty white, green-dotted bells dangle in groups of three. Midspring blooming. In mild climates may bloom again, November to winter.
Plant hardiness: Zones 4–9; to zone 3 with winter protection.
Soil needs: Moist, clay, rich in organic matter. Fertility: Rich. 6.0–8.0 pH.
Planting: Prefers shade part of the day, handles more sun in wet soil. 2 in. (50 mm) apart.
Care: Plant bulbs 4 in. (10 cm) deep in autumn. Keep moist throughout growing season. Blooms only when well established.
Features: Good choice for massing along edges, shaded corners.

Common name: Sprite, Pink
Scientific name: *Rotala rotundifolia*
Habitat/Size: Shoreline, shallow-depth marginal. Grows to 4 in. (10 cm.) tall. Spreading.
Description: Deciduous perennial. Submerged, the plant grows erect. On the shoreline, it is a clumping ground cover. Opposite, small, egg-shaped leaves, pale green above and white to reddish beneath. Exposed leaves are dark green. Small pink to violet flowers. Summer to autumn blooming.
Plant hardiness: Zones 10–11.
Soil needs: Moist. Warm water. Fertility: Average. 6.0–7.0 pH.
Planting: Full sun to partial shade. 1 ft. (30 cm.) apart. Submerge 6–12 in. (15–30 cm) deep.
Care: Will not flower if water is too deep. Propagate from cuttings.
Features: Good choice for backgrounds, massing in small-space water gardens.

Common name: Sundew
Scientific name: *Drosera* species
Habitat/Size: Shoreline. Small size varies by species.
Description: About 100 species of mostly perennials. Rosettes of leaf blades have sticky, insect-trapping hairs spangling the rounded ends. Small blossoms on a slender stalk, white, purple, pink, yellow. Summer blooming.
Plant hardiness: Zones 8–10.
Soil needs: Mix of peat and sand. Fertility: Poor. 6.0 pH.
Planting: Full sun. 1 ft. (30 cm) apart.
Care: Grow from seed or leaf cuttings. Needs generous water when growing, ideally from below ground. Cold-winter species form winter-resting buds. Needs vary widely by species.
Features: Good choice for locations that can be viewed. The easiest to grow have forked leaves. *D. intermedia* and *D. linearis* tolerate alkaline conditions. Some North American natives.

Common name: Sweet Flag
Scientific name: *Acorus Calamus*
Habitat/Size: Shoreline, shallow-depth marginal. Grows to 6 ft. (1.8 m) tall and wide.
Description: Deciduous perennial. Bold, vertical, bright green, crimp-edged irislike leaf blades grow in clumps from rhizomes. Produces greenish brown flower only when grown in water; flower stalk is shorter than leaves. Foliage is aromatic.
Plant hardiness: Zones 3–10.
Soil needs: Constantly moist, loam, rich in organic matter. Fertility: Rich. 6.0–8.0 pH.
Planting: Full sun. 3 ft. (90 cm) apart. Submerge 6 in. (15 cm) deep.
Care: Plant 2-in. (50-mm) sections of rhizome in spring. Divide crowded clumps every 2–4 years in autumn. Sow fresh seed in autumn.
Features: Good choice for accent or border of informal garden ponds. Striped leaves of variegated type add interest. Sweet aroma.

Common name: Sweet Flag, Dwarf; Grassy-leaved Sweet Flag
Scientific name: *Acorus gramineus*
Habitat/Size: Shoreline, deep-depth marginal. Grows to 18 in. (45 cm) long.
Description: Semievergreen perennial. Low-growing fans of narrow, glossy, grasslike leaves spread by rhizomes. Variegated forms spread more slowly.
Plant hardiness: Zones 3–11.
Soil needs: Constantly moist, loam, rich in organic matter. Fertility: Rich. 6.0–8.0 pH.
Planting: Full sun. 1 ft. (30 cm) apart. Submerge up to 10 in. (25 cm) deep.
Care: Plant 2-in. (50-mm) sections of rhizome in spring. Divide crowded clumps every 2–4 years in autumn. Sow fresh seed in autumn.
Features: Good choice for ground cover. Cultivars offer yellow and striped leaves. Golden-leaved varieties such as 'Oboruzuki' and 'Ogon' stand out among garden greens.

Common name: Thalia, Powdery; Hardy Canna
Scientific name: *Thalia dealbata*
Habitat/Size: Shallow-depth marginal, deep-depth marginal. Grows 3–6 ft. (90–180 cm) tall, 2 ft. (60 cm) wide.
Description: Evergreen perennial. Tall stems bear stiff glossy leaves at intervals. Grapelike clusters, lavender inner flowers emerge from pale jade bracts. Widely branching flower heads bloom from early spring into autumn. Attractive seed heads follow.
Plant hardiness: Zones 6–10.
Soil needs: Moist, loam, rich in organic matter. Fertility: Rich. 6.0–8.0 pH.
Planting: Full sun to partial shade. 3 ft. (90 cm) apart. Submerge 6–18 in. (15–45 cm) deep.
Care: Plant seeds in spring, divide in spring or summer. Remove fading foliage. If roots are protected from freezing, can survive to 20°F (7°C).
Features: Good choice for accents, backgrounds. North American native.

Common name: Venus's Flytrap
Scientific name: *Dionaea muscipula*
Habitat/Size: Shoreline. Grows to 8 in. (20 cm) wide.
Description: Carnivorus perennial. Rosettes of vivid light green stems sport bright pink, fringed fly-trapping lobes. With enough protein in diet, produces white flowers. June blooming.
Plant hardiness: Zones 8–10.
Soil needs: Moist, porous, peaty. Fertility: Average. 6.0–8.0 pH.
Planting: Full sun for best color, faster trapping action. 10 in. (25 cm) apart.
Care: Keep constantly moist; reduce water when growth slows. Tolerates temperatures just above freezing. May go dormant in winter. Stimulate new trap growth by pinching new flowers and spent traps. Slug, botrytis susceptible.
Features: Good choice for self-contained gardens near seating area for entertainment value. When an insect triggers a sensing hair twice, the trap closes. Try feeding a bit of meat or cheese every now and then. Eastern U.S. native.

Common name: Wake Robin; Trillium
Scientific name: *Trillium* species
Habitat/Size: Shoreline. Grows 6–24 in. (15–60 cm).
Description: About 30 species of clumping perennials of the lily family. Long pointed oval leaves, 2–6 in. (50–150 mm) long, in whorls of three at the top of the stem. One 3-petal flower 3 in. (80 mm) wide rises from the center of leaves. Greenish white aging to rose, deep maroon. Spring blooming.
Plant hardiness: Zones 3–9.
Soil needs: Moist, well-drained. Fertility: Rich. 6.5–7.0 pH.
Planting: Partial to full shade. 5–8 in. (13–20 cm) apart.
Care: Easy. Thrives with infrequent watering in shade conditions. Will self sow.
Features: Good choice for shade areas around water feature in woodland gardens.

*I have often thought that if heaven had given me
a choice of my position and calling,
it should have been on a rich spot of earth, well watered...
No occupation is so delightful to me as the culture of the earth,
and no culture comparable to that of the garden.*

THOMAS JEFFERSON

Common name: Water Clover, Variegated
Scientific name: *Marsilea mutica* 'Variegata'
Habitat/Size: Shallow-depth marginal, deep-depth marginal. Grows 3–14 in. (75–350 mm) tall.
Description: Aquatic fern. Delicate four-leaf cloverlike leaves with attractive two-tone markings float on water surface.
Plant hardiness: Zones 6–11.
Soil needs: Wet, rich in organic matter. Fertility: Rich. 5.0–6.5 pH.
Planting: Full sun to partial shade. 16 in. (40 cm) apart. Submerge 3–12 in. (75–300 mm) over crown
Care: Ideal water temperature is 68–72°F (20–22°C). Divide rhizomes to control growth.
Features: Good choice for combining with large water lily pads. Plant will spread twice as wide as container. An ancient species, primitive fern.

Common name: Watercress
Scientific name: *Nasturtium officinale*
Habitat/Size: Shallow-depth marginal. Grows 8–30 in. (20–75 cm) long.
Description: Perennial. Branching, creeping stems bear clusters of round leaflets, tiny white flowers. March to November blooming.
Plant hardiness: Zones 3–11.
Soil needs: Moist, sandy, rich in organic matter. Fertility: Rich. 7.2 pH.
Planting: Full sun to partial shade, flowing water. 6 in. (15 cm) apart. Submerge to crown.
Care: Hardy in clean water, very sensitive to pollutants. Avoid pesticides and herbicides if growing for food. Harvest sparingly the first year.
Features: Good choice for streams, watercourses. Will trail from water to shoreline, blending feature to garden, covering liner edge. Harvest to add peppery zest plus vitamins and minerals to salads, soups, and sandwiches.

Common name: Water Fern; Water Spangles
Scientific name: *Salvinia* species
Habitat/Size: Surface floater. Grows 6–10 in. (15–25 cm) long.
Description: About 10 species of free-floating deciduous perennial ferns. Dark green, coin-shaped leaflets crowd the slender stems of this rootless fern.
Plant hardiness: Zones 10–11.
Soil needs: 6.0–8.0 pH.
Planting: Full sun. Warm, still water.
Care: Easy in warm conditions. Branches break off and grow; but seldom produces spores in water features. Clear surface of loose branches to prevent pump and filter clogs.
Features: Good choice for fish ponds, indoor features, greenhouses. Small leafy form contrasts well with water lily pads. Spreads fast in warm water, forming mat that shades and cools pond, shelters fish. Usually goes dormant in winter. Tends to be invasive in tropical and subtropical waters.

Common name: Water Figwort; Water Betony
Scientific name: *Scrophularia auriculata*
Habitat/Size: Shoreline. Grows 2–3 ft. (60–90 cm) tall.
Description: Strongly scented perennial shrub. Upright, 4-sided stems bear multiple crinkled, curved leaves 2–10 in. (50–250 mm) long at intervals. Small green-and-purple flowers cluster at the tips. Grown for attractive foliage.
Plant hardiness: Zones 5–10.
Soil needs: Moist, well-drained. Fertility: Average. 6.0–8.0 pH.
Planting: Full sun to partial shade. Allow room for clumps to spread without crowding.
Care: Frost-hardy. Plant autumn to spring. May self-sow.
Features: Good choice for accents in woodland gardens, cut foliage. Attracts bees. North American native.

Common name: Water Hawthorn; Cape Pondweed
Scientific name: *Aponogeton distachyus*
Habitat/Size: Deep-depth marginal. Grows 2 in. (50 mm) above the water, 1 ft. (30 cm) wide.
Description: Tender perennial. Spreading across water surface, rosettes of stiff, narrow, leathery leaves angle upward, encircling short stalks of vanilla-scented, twin-branched white flower clusters.
Plant hardiness: Zones 8–11.
Soil needs: Clay loam, rich in organic matter. Fertility: Rich. 6.0–8.0 pH.
Planting: Full sun to partial shade. 1–2 ft. (30–60 cm) apart. Submerge 10–24 in. (25–60 cm) deep.
Care: Keep fresh seeds moist until planted. Propagate by seed, division in spring.
Features: Good alternative choice to lilies. Blooming times vary by climate: spring, autumn in temperate areas; summer in cold-winter zones; cool weather where summers are hottest.

Common name: Water Hyacinth
Scientific name: *Eichhornia crassipes*
Habitat/Size: Surface floater. Grows 2–12 in. (50–300 mm) tall, 2–10 in. (50–250 cm) wide.
Description: Semievergreen. Highly attractive, glossy leaf rosettes on inflated bladders form floating mat. Delicate, hyacinth-like flower spikes rise above. Each lilac blue flower has one yellow-spotted petal.
Plant hardiness: Zones 9–11.
Soil needs: Water 60–90°F (15–30°C). 5.5–9.0 pH.
Planting: Full sun, sheltered from wind.
Care: Set plant on water surface after last frost. In cold climates, overwinter in containers of sandy loam mix, kept moist, with good light, at 59–68°F (15–20°C). Clean dropped bladders from bottom of feature to prevent pump and filter clogs. Control growth by removing runners.
Features: Good choice for fish ponds; it shades water, reduces algae growth, absorbs fish waste. Roots provide a fish nursery, and turtles will eat all parts. Cultivation is prohibited in some regions.

Common name: Water Lettuce
Scientific name: *Pistia stratiotes*
Habitat/Size: Surface floater. Grows 2–8 in. (50–200 mm) high and wide.
Description: Deciduous perennial. Lush, blue green rosettes of ribbed leaves float on spongy submerged bladders. Floats or anchors on bottom.
Plant hardiness: Zones 10–11.
Soil needs: Water 66–72°F (19–22°C). Fertility: Lime-free. 6.5–7.0 pH.
Planting: Full sun, protect from hot sun.
Care: Set into water. It rapidly covers surface and can smother other plants. Control overgrowth by removing excess. Clean dropped bladders from bottom of feature to prevent pump and filter clogs. Divide plantlets in summer.
Features: Good choice for fish ponds, it shades water, reduces algae growth, offers cover for young fish, which feed on the feathery roots. A serious nuisance in some southern U.S. states; cultivation is prohibited in some regions.

WATER LILY

Water lilies are the quintessential aquatic plant. In addition to their soothing beauty and fragrance, lilies shade and cool the water and offer cover for fish.

The water lily family—or Nymphaeaceae—is made up of seven cultivated genera and about 65 species of perennial aquatic plants: *Brasenia, Cabomba, Euryale, Nelumbo, Nuphar, Nymphaea,* and *Victoria.* There are cultivars available in a broad range of colors and sizes. All of these water lilies fall into two general selection and care categories: hardy and tropical. Hardy lilies thrive year-round in an outdoor pond to zone 4, as long as the water remains unfrozen. In colder climates, move the container inside to shelter through the winter. Tropical lilies require warmer temperatures.

Tropical water lilies are either day bloomers or night bloomers that open at dusk and close by noon. All are fragrant. The night bloomers have an intense, haunting aroma that lures pollinating insects. If you're gone all day and look forward to summer evenings by the pond, treat yourself to at least one night-bloomer. Both types need water at least 70°F (21°C), although older plants can tolerate somewhat cooler water. Grow as annuals, remove and store the rhizomes before the first frost and plant again in spring, or move the container to a sunny greenhouse. Tropicals reward these extra efforts with lavish blooming unmatched by the hardy lilies, often well into autumn.

Plant new lily rhizomes in spring, just as growth begins. Place in containers, in rich, heavy clay soil covered with gravel, leaving the growing tip exposed. Hardy lilies need a wide container so their shallow roots can spread. Add fertilizer granules at planting and every 1–3 months, depending on the individual plant. Submerge when the water reaches 55–60°F (13–15°C) for hardy lilies and 70°F (21°C) for tropicals, 6–18 in. (15–45 cm) over the growing tip. Increase depth gradually as the plant matures.

You'll need to divide rootbound plants every few years, annually in zones 8–11. Spring is the ideal time; it can be done later, but you'll miss out on weeks of flowering.

Most water lilies bloom for just 3 days, opening and closing each day, with strongest fragrance on day one. You can keep a cut flower open by carefully dripping hot wax onto the inner base of each petal; the hardened wax prevents closing. Cut them on the first day, with 1 ft. (30 cm) of stem, and place in water to within 1 in. (25 mm) of a hardy lily's blossom, 3 in. (75 mm) of a tropical's. It will last 3 or 4 days.

Common name: Water Lily

Scientific name: *Nymphaea* species

Habitat/Size: Deep-depth submersible. Grows 4 ft. (1.2 m) spread, leaves 9–10 in. (23–25 cm) wide. Flowers 2–10 in. (50–250 mm) across.

Description: About 35 species of deciduous perennials, grown as annuals. Tropical and hardy. Leaves mature from purple to green. Flowers in white, yellow, shades of pink, and red. Summer blooming.

Plant hardiness: Zones 4–6.

Soil needs: Clay, rich in organic matter. Fertility: Rich. 6–8 pH.

Planting: Full sun. 4 ft. (1.2 m) apart. Submerge 6–18 in. (15–45 cm) deep.

Care: Easy when conditions are met.

Features: Good choice for a medium to large pond. Best in cooler northern climates. Where summers are hot, fewer flowers are produced and the petals may blacken the second day.

Common name: Water Lily, Amazon; Royal Water Lily
Scientific name: *Victoria amazonica*
Habitat/Size: Deep-water submersible. Grows leaves to 6 ft. (1.8 m) wide, flowers to 1 ft. (30 cm) wide.
Description: Perennial often grown as an annual. Quickly reaches spectacular size. Night-blooming with intense pineapple fragrance; turns from cream the first evening to pink, rose, or purple the second.
Plant hardiness: Zones 10–11.
Soil needs: Loam, high in organic matter. Fertility: Average. 6.0–8.0 pH.
Planting: Full sun. Still water over 80°F (27°C) to bloom. Plant seed from midwinter to early spring and immerse container in water kept at 85–90°F (29–32°C). When leaves sprout, submerge to 18 in. (45 cm) deep. Final placement 3 ft. (90 cm) deep.
Care: Feed mature plants slow-release fertilizer.
Features: Good choice for accents. Matures at 7 months. Flowers bloom one at a time. Sharp prickles cover the stems, undersides of leaves, and seed heads.

Common name: Water-parsley, Variegated
Scientific name: *Oenanthe sarmentosa*
Habitat/Size: Shallow-depth marginal. Grows 1–5 ft. (30–150 cm) tall. Spreading.
Description: Evergreen perennial. Opposite, green leaves. Roots as it grows, filling between rocks. Minute clusters of white flowers. Summer blooming.
Plant hardiness: Zones 4–9.
Soil needs: Moist. Fertility: Average. 7.0 pH.
Planting: Full sun to partial shade. Submerge 1–4 in. (25–100 mm).
Care: Foliage may turn pink in cool weather.
Features: Good choice for edges. Plant in bunches. 'Flamingo' is dwarf cultivar for small-space gardens. Western North American native.

Common name: Water Plantain
Scientific name: *Alisma Plantago-aquatica*
Habitat/Size: Deep-depth marginal. Grows to 3 ft. (90 cm) tall, flower stems 8–40 in. (20–100 cm) tall.
Description: Deciduous perennial. Rosettes of gray green to deep green leaves reach 6 in. (15 cm) above surface. Clouds of tiny white to purplish white flowers. Summer blooming.
Plant hardiness: Zones 5–10.
Soil needs: Wet, rich in organic matter. Fertility: Average. 6.0–8.0 pH.
Planting: Full sun. 3 ft. (90 cm) apart. Submerge to 10 in. (25 cm) deep.
Care: Easy. Immerse ripe seeds in shallow water to germinate before planting in containers. Deadhead flowers to prevent self-sowing. Remove faded leaves in autumn. Propagate by seed in summer, division in spring.
Features: Good choice for cool, damp locations. Languishes in hot, dry sun.

Common name: Water Snowflake; Banana Lily; Floating-heart

Scientific name: *Nymphoides* species

Habitat/Size: Deciduous perennial. Shallow-depth marginal, deep-depth marginal. Grows to 6 ft. (1.8 m) spread, leaves 3–12 in. (75–300 mm) wide.

Description: Has the look of a miniature water lily. Different species have variegated lily-pad leaves, round or heart-shaped. Finely fringed white, lemon yellow, or poppy orange flowers ¾ in. (19 mm) wide.

Plant hardiness: Zones 5–11, varies by species.

Soil needs: Clay loam. Fertility: Average. 6.0–8.0 pH.

Planting: Full sun to partial shade. 3 ft. (90 cm) apart. Submerge 1–24 in. (25–600 mm) over crown.

Care: Immerse ripe seeds in shallow water to germinate before planting in containers. Divide in spring or root plantlets in autumn. Grow tropical species as annuals or overwinter tubers indoors. Avoid algae control agents such as formalin.

Features: Good choice for small water features, self-contained gardens.

Common name: Wintergreen

Scientific name: *Gaultheria procumbens*

Habitat/Size: Shoreline. Grows to 6 in. (15 cm) tall.

Description: Aromatic evergreen with tiny, bell-shaped white flowers tinged with pink bloom followed by bright red, mint-flavored berries. Thick leathery leaves 1–2 in. (25–50 mm) long grow on woody stalks, turn bronze in autumn. Summer blooming.

Plant hardiness: Zones 5–8.

Soil needs: Moist, well-drained, humus-rich. Fertility: Moderately rich. 4.0–6.0 pH.

Planting: Partial to full shade. 1–2 ft. (30–60 cm) apart.

Care: Water regularly.

Features: Good choice for shade areas around water feature. Original source of wintergreen flavor. North American native.

Common name: Wishbone Flower; Bluewings

Scientific name: *Torenia Fournieri*

Habitat/Size: Shoreline. Grows 10–12 in. (25–30 cm).

Description: Annual. Oval, toothed leaves. Purple blue, white with purplish spots, pink, or white with a yellow throat flowers 1 in. (25 mm) wide. Spring to frost blooming.

Plant hardiness: Zones 4–11.

Soil needs: Sand or loam, very moist, well-drained. Fertility: Rich. 7.0 pH.

Planting: Partial to light shade. 6–8 in. (15–20 cm) apart. Start seeds indoors 6–8 weeks before final frost date. Plant year-round in frost-free areas.

Care: Water regularly, deeply. Pinch back to promote bushy growth. Propagate from seed.

Features: Good choice for above-ground containers, beds, borders, edge of water feature, greenhouses. Often used as a substitute for pansy.

The United States Department of Agriculture [USDA] Plant Hardiness Zone system provides a general guide to growing conditions in North America. It divides the continent into 11 zones based on the average minimum annual temperatures within each zone. The USDA system has been adapted to other areas of the world [see USDA Plant Hardiness Around the World, pg. 116–117]. The zones roughly predict which plants will survive in a given area. Because weather varies from year to year, the actual minimum temperatures may be lower or higher than indicated on the plant hardiness map.

When you're planning for a new water feature on your site, use all of the information contained in the plant hardiness zone maps to guide your plant selections. First find your locale on a map, then identify your zone by comparing its color to the legend. Many aquatic plant growers include zone information on their plant tags for your convenience.

Remember, aquatic plants grow best in zones where they've adapted fully to the climate. It's possible that plants from warmer hardiness zones than yours may live and bloom in your water feature during a series of warm-winter years, only to fail when a cold year is experienced again.

Your major concern in addition to plant hardiness zone will be the first and last frost dates in your area [see Approximate Frost-free Dates, pg. 116]. The average first and last frost dates for your area are general guidelines, however, and should be used subject to experience and advice.

Moreover, neither zone maps nor frost charts can account for the effects of thermal belts, nearby bodies of water, topography, and other factors that create microclimates within zones. Only careful observation will give you an accurate picture of climatic conditions in your own backyard.

> **Climate and microclimate govern plant choices when water features are planned and planted**

Plant Hardiness Around the World

Each water feature is a microcosm of a real world environment. It quickly expands to include many animals and insects, plus many new plants that arrive as seeds, spores, hidden as hitchhikers with other plants or carried to the feature by visiting birds.

USDA Plant Hardiness Around the World
North America

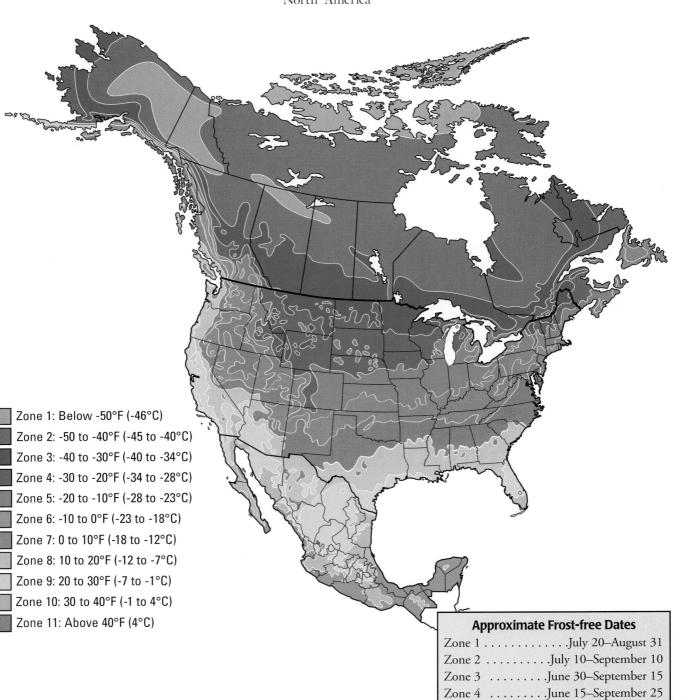

Zone 1: Below -50°F (-46°C)

Zone 2: -50 to -40°F (-45 to -40°C)

Zone 3: -40 to -30°F (-40 to -34°C)

Zone 4: -30 to -20°F (-34 to -28°C)

Zone 5: -20 to -10°F (-28 to -23°C)

Zone 6: -10 to 0°F (-23 to -18°C)

Zone 7: 0 to 10°F (-18 to -12°C)

Zone 8: 10 to 20°F (-12 to -7°C)

Zone 9: 20 to 30°F (-7 to -1°C)

Zone 10: 30 to 40°F (-1 to 4°C)

Zone 11: Above 40°F (4°C)

Approximate Frost-free Dates

Zone 1	July 20–August 31
Zone 2	July 10–September 10
Zone 3	June 30–September 15
Zone 4	June 15–September 25
Zone 5	May 25–October 10
Zone 6	May 15–October 20
Zone 7	April 25–November 1
Zone 8	April 15–November 10
Zone 9	March 15–November 15
Zone 10	February 10–December 10
Zone 11	Frost-free All Year

USDA Plant Hardiness Around the World
Australia

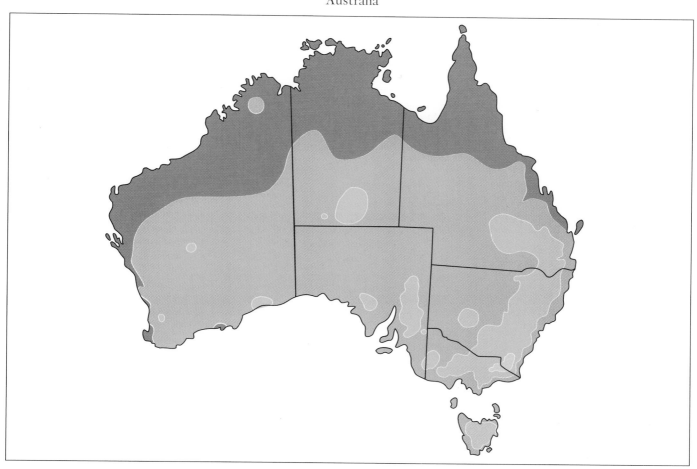

South Africa

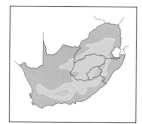

New Zealand

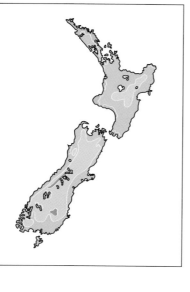

Europe

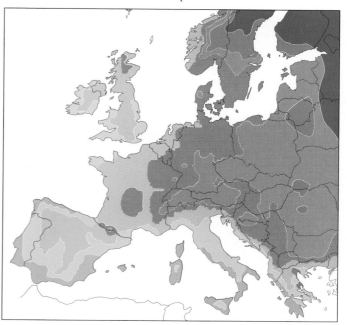

ON-LINE   INDEX

I N D E X

INDEX